The *Song of Songs*

LIVES OF GREAT RELIGIOUS BOOKS

FORTHCOMING

The *Song of Songs*

A BIOGRAPHY

Ilana Pardes

PRINCETON UNIVERSITY PRESS

Princeton and Oxford

Copyright © 2019 by Princeton University Press

Published by Princeton University Press
41 William Street, Princeton, New Jersey 08540
6 Oxford Street, Woodstock, Oxfordshire OX20 1TR

press.princeton.edu

LCCN: 2018955057
ISBN 0-691-14606-5

British Library Cataloging-in-Publication Data is available

Editorial: Fred Appel and Thalia Leaf
Production Editorial: Debbie Tegarden
Text Design: Lorraine Doneker
Jacket Design: Lorraine Doneker
Jacket Art: Anna Ruth Henriques, *Song of Songs* chapter 3, 1995
Production: Jacquie Poirier
Publicity: Tayler Lord and Kathryn Stevens
Copyeditor: Sarah Vogelsong

This book has been composed in Garamond Premier Pro

Printed on acid-free paper. ∞

Printed in the United States of America

10 9 8 7 6 5 4 3 2 1

For Itamar

dodi tsah ve-'adom dagul me-revava

CONTENTS

ILLUSTRATIONS

ACKNOWLEDGMENTS

I've been fortunate to have had many fellow travelers in the course of writing this book. I am greatly indebted to Robert Alter, Miri Avissar, Leora Batnitzky, Ron Hendel, Vivian Liska, Yosefa Raz, Naomi Seidman, Rachel Wamsley, and Steve Weitzman for reading the entire manuscript and offering many valuable suggestions. I have also benefited from the insights of many other friends and colleagues at different stations along the way: Avishai Bar-Asher, Rita Copeland, Melila Eshed-Helner, Luis Girón-Negrón, Ruth HaCohen, Yisca Harani, Galit Hasan-Rokem, Or Hasson, Moshe Idel, Rut Kaniel Kara-Ivanov, Ofek Kehila, Chana Kronfeld, Yonatan Moss, Elaine Pagels, Ishay Rosen-Zvi, Jonathan Sheehan, Shai Skunda, Shira Wolosky, and Ariel Zinder.

I am indebted to the astute students of two seminars I gave at the Hebrew University on "The Song of Songs as Cultural Text" in 2013 and 2015. In the fall of 2012, while beginning work on this book, I had the pleasure of teaching a seminar on the Song of Songs in the Department of Comparative Literature and Jewish Studies at Harvard University. I put the final touches on the book at Princeton University in the fall of 2017 as a fellow of the Humanities Council. For financial support, I am indebted to the Israel Science Foundation and to internal grants from the Hebrew University.

Special thanks go to Fred Appel, my editor at Princeton University Press, for inviting me to contribute a volume to *Lives of Great Religious Books* and for his much-appreciated and thoughtful advice throughout. I am greatly indebted to Thalia Leaf of Princeton University Press for her helpful comments. I'm also grateful to the anonymous reader of Princeton University Press for his hard work and many perceptive suggestions. Many thanks go to Batnadiv Hakarmi-Weinberg for her insightful input in the initial stages of writing. David Lobenstine stepped into the picture at a later stage and encouraged me to explore new modes of writing. I cannot thank him enough for his inspiring editorial work.

My family—Itamar, Keren, and Eyal—have been an incredible source of love and encouragement. This book on the ultimate song of love is dedicated to Itamar.

June 2018

LIVES OF GREAT RELIGIOUS BOOKS

The *Song of Songs*

"Draw Me After You, Let Us Run"

The Song of Songs opens with a craving to be kissed: "Let him kiss me with the kisses of his mouth, / for your loving is better than wine . . . / poured oil is your name" (1:2–3).[1] The beloved craves not just kisses, but luscious kisses. The kisses she longs for hover between intoxicating wine and perfumed oil, embodying an exhilarating welter of senses—taste, touch, and smell. Sound, too, joins this sensual celebration: a repeated "sh" rustle begins with the title of the Song of Songs, *shir ha-shirim*, and flows onto many of the words that follow, among them *neshikot*, "kisses."[2]

There is something dreamy about these opening lines of the Song. It isn't quite clear from whence the voice of the beloved emerges or to whom she is speaking. She first speaks about her loved one in the third person to unidentified addressees—"Let him kiss me"—but then switches to the second person as she hails her loved one more intimately: "For your loving is better than wine." The bewildering dream logic deepens in the next sequence:

Draw me after you, let us run.

The king has brought me to his chamber.

Let us be glad and rejoice in you.

Let us extol your loving beyond wine.

Rightly do they love you. (1:4)

Is the beloved in the intimate realm of her lover's chamber or outdoors at a feast surrounded by those whom she calls upon to rejoice in her love? Is her lover actually a king, or is he made larger than life by her loving gaze? And is it the maddening power of love that makes her imagine the entire world as equally enamored of him as she is? It is a dream zone—nothing is completely discernable, everything is deeply felt. We move with unparalleled speed from one metaphor to another, from one site to another, with no distinctions between inside and outside, no temporal transitions, and no need for explanation.

What gives this dreamscape a special sense of vitality and urgency is its imperative mood.[3] "Draw me after you, let us run," demands the beloved. It is not a negotiable request but one that must be embraced at once. The time of love is an ever-rolling present that allows for no restful meandering. One must hurry, dash off, move ahead.

This downpour of imperatives is also addressed to us as readers of the Song. We are not invited into the world of the Song with a peaceful gesture. Rather, we are urged by the imperative of love to join the wild pace of amorous dialogues and dreams. The beloved draws and is drawn, and we're called upon to run in her footsteps.

Readers have indeed been drawn to the Song for many centuries. Rabbis, church fathers, mystics, nuns, scholars, poets, writers, musicians, artists, and readers from all walks of life have been charmed by the Song and have extolled it as the ultimate song of love, endorsing the Song's own definition of itself as *shir hashirim*, the song that surpasses all other songs. Whether searching for divine love, earthly love, or both, readers have turned to the Song as the definitive expression of their amorous experiences, as an infinitely rich turf upon which to explore the diverse facets of love.

Who could have written this ultimate love poem? The Song was traditionally attributed to King Solomon, the king whose name is evoked in the first verse—"The Song of Songs, which is Solomon's" (1:1)—the poet-king who allegedly composed "a thousand and five songs" (1 Kings 5:12), the only king whose wisdom was so grand and all-encompassing (even the language of trees and beasts was within his reach) that he could venture to grapple with the greatest riddle of all: love. That Solomon had seven hundred women and three hundred concubines probably contributed to his reputation as an expert on love.[4]

The assumption that Solomon was the Song's author has been regarded as untenable ever since the Enlightenment. Most scholars today define the Song as an anthology of love poems, composed and culled by sundry hands over many centuries. The Song's beginnings may have been early, possibly even during Solomon's reign in the tenth century BCE, but the final stages of its composition and editing must have been late—somewhere between the fifth and fourth centuries BCE—given that there are many terms pertaining to the later strata of biblical Hebrew or borrowed from Persian and Greek.[5]

This collection of love poems revolves around a dialogue between two young lovers: the Shulamite, as the beloved is called, and her nameless lover.[6] There is something utterly refreshing in the frank celebration of love that is found in the passionate exchanges of the two. Nowhere else in the Bible are bodily parts—hair, nose, eyes, lips, tongue, breasts, thighs—set on a pedestal; nowhere else are the sensual pleasures of love—tastes, colors, sounds, and perfumes—relished with such joy; nowhere else is sexual desire spelled out with so much verve. And yet sexuality is never blatant in the Song. Instead we find a nuanced combination of audacity, innocence, and decorum, made possible by a spectacular metaphoric web that allows the two lovers to be direct and indirect at once.

Both lovers are masters of metaphor. If much of the love poetry of antiquity (and beyond) sets male lovers on stage as the agents of courting, here we find a strikingly egalitarian amorous dialogue between two virtuoso speakers who woo each other while juggling a plethora of metaphors and similes from different realms. They liken each other to roses, trees, gazelles, doves, goats, the moon, the sun, a crimson thread, perfumes, gold, precious stones, locks, walls, and towers. No figure of speech seems to suffice in depicting love.

Metaphors pertaining to natural landscapes are the most prevalent. Much of the beauty of the love scenes in the Song derives from the lovers' evocations of the plant world. Consider the following sequence:

I am the rose of Sharon,
 the lily of the valley.
—Like a lily among the thorns
 so is my friend among the young women.
—Like a quince tree among the trees of the forest
 so is my lover among the young men.
In its shade I delighted to sit
 and its fruit was sweet to my taste. (2:1–3)

The Shulamite celebrates her beauty without hesitation as she likens herself to a rose and then to a lily. Biblical poetry is not based on systematic metrics or rhyming but rather on parallelisms between two (and at times three) components of a line. In this case, we have a classic semantic parallelism between two versets: "I am the rose of Sharon" and "the lily of the valley." It may seem redundant to place two different metaphors of flowers one right after the other. One may also wonder about the inconsistency: Can the beloved be both a rose and a lily? But there is nothing arbitrary in this parallelism, for the enumeration of two flowers heightens the Song's overriding sense of exuberance: metaphors flow or overflow, one after the other, incessant as love.[7]

Figurative language is an intrinsic element of courtship in the Song and is continuously made seductive as the lovers respond to each other. The lover adopts the beloved's metaphoric choice—or rather picks up the thread of the second metaphor, the lily (*shoshana*)—and adds his own note of admiration by elaborating on the singularity of the lily, turning all the other maidens into thorns. Following her lover's comparative perspective, the Shulamite hails him as unique among the young men, much as a fruit tree stands out among the trees of the wood. She then plunges into this imaginary landscape and makes it semiconcrete by sitting under a quince tree ("apple tree" in the King James Version) and relishing its shade and sweet fruit. But is she actually sitting under a tree, or should her depiction of eating the ravishing fruit be construed as a provocative double entendre through which she envisions the pleasures of lovemaking?

Once the lovers are cast in the roles of flowers and trees, every call to go out to explore the delights of springtime entails a craving to savor their own metaphorical blossoming as humans, ripe for the act of love. Scenes of spring are both the literal settings in which the lovers meet and a favorite figurative component of their amorous dialogue, a lovers' code of sorts.

The lovers, who love and feel loved to the depth of their being, are the protagonists of the Song, but other interlocutors appear occasionally, some unidentified and others belonging to known groups. The daughters of Jerusalem, a female chorus of sorts with whom the

Shulamite shares her inner tumult, are the most prominent group of addressees. But there are also two rather hostile male groups—the Shulamite's brothers and the watchmen of the city walls—who try to set limits on, or even block, the beloved's amorous pursuits.

The abundance of dialogues between the lovers as well as between the Shulamite and her interlocutors has led some readers—as different as the church father Origen and modern biblical scholars—to define the Song as a drama with identifiable scenes. Such readings are attuned to the performative dimension of the Song's language of love, but any attempt to find a coherent line of action or a clearly defined drama in this ancient anthology of love poems is ultimately strained. The division into eight chapters is quite arbitrary and does not rely on clear poetic demarcations. Poems emerge out of nowhere, merge with one another, or end abruptly. And the lovers, like their poems, appear and disappear unexpectedly. We can follow them as they court each other in every imaginable way, but their love story remains patently fragmentary.

Even the location in which love blooms cannot be pinned down. We begin in the royal chambers and then, for no apparent reason, shift to the vineyards, after which we find ourselves in pastoral pastures by shepherds' huts and in fields. Some of the subsequent scenes are more urban in character, taking place either in lush gardens or in the dwellings and streets of Jerusalem.

Within this stream of ever-shifting settings, the two lovers search for each other via a flirtatious hide-and-seek. At times, the lover peers through the windows like a stag in search of his beloved (2:9); at other times, he tries to lure her out, as if she were a dove hidden in a rock's crevices (2:14). More often, it is the Shulamite who most forcefully embodies amorous longing, rushing as she does, time and again, to look for her loved one.

The closest we get to a plot within the world of this amorous search is in chapter 5, the navel of the poem. Set in Jerusalem, this nocturnal episode begins in the beloved's abode. The semi-sleeping Shulamite hears her loved one knocking and hastens to speak to him behind the door.

> I was asleep but my heart was awake:
>> Hark! my lover knocks.
> —Open for me, my sister, my friend,
>> my dove, my perfect one.
> For my head is drenched with dew,
>> my locks with the drops of the night . . .
> My lover pulled back his hand from the latch,
>> and my heart raced within me.
> I rose to open for my lover.
>> My hands dripped myrrh
> and my fingers liquid myrrh,
>> over the handles of the bolt.
> I opened for my lover,
>> but my lover had slipped off, was gone . . .

I sought him but did not find him.

I called him but he did not answer. (5:2–6)

It is here that the dreamlike quality of the text, intimated from the very beginning, becomes palpable. The exquisite verse "I was asleep but my heart was awake" (*'ani yeshena ve-libbi 'er*) underscores the paradoxical experience of dreams, split as they are between passive sleep and a wakefulness that may exceed that of daytime. But it is also a reminder of love's overwhelming capacity to rouse, to engulf—in emotional spheres as well as bodily zones—whether one is awake or asleep.

The Shulamite is beckoned by her lover to rise and "open to [him]," but no door is mentioned explicitly, which is why the lover's request calls for several readings. Is the lover, whose "head is drenched with dew," asking his beloved to unlock a literal door, or is he trying to gain access to her heart and body? Once again, literal sites lend themselves to a figurative reading. Nothing remains purely literal in this dripping dialogue "over the handles of the bolt," nothing escapes erotic coloring.

When the Shulamite finally unlocks the door, her lover is no longer there.[8] Longing for him, she desperately ventures into the city streets at night to search for her loved one. The watchmen of the walls find the meandering beloved and beat her, pulling off the shawl that she wears. Is this an actual encounter, or has her dream turned into a nightmare? Whether real or imaginary, no watchmen or walls can stop the Shulamite.

She now calls upon the daughters of Jerusalem to join her in her search and adjures them to pass on to her absent lover one urgent message: that she is lovesick (*holat ahava 'ani*). The intensity of love may be more of a malady than a cure.

This hint of a plot fades as we switch to a sequence of exchanges between the beloved and the daughters of Jerusalem. To their question, "How is your lover more than another . . . / that thus you made us vow?" (5:9), she responds with a detailed and laudatory depiction of her lover's body parts:

> —My lover is shining white and ruddy . . .
> His head is purest gold,
> > his locks are curls
> > > black as a raven . . .
> His thighs are ivory pillars
> set on pedestals of gold. (Song 5:10–15)

What follows is no scene in which the two lovers unite with joy, commenting on their painful separation. Rather, the lover appears again only in 6:4, as if he were never gone, and delivers a descriptive poem of his own, with glorifying accounts of the beloved's body. There is an associative flow but no attempt to fill in narrative lacunas. The final chapters of the Song offer no clear-cut denouement, exhibiting a similar mélange of snatches of dialogue intertwined with descriptive poems.

Were the Song's editors blind to the unruly character of this anthology of love poems? We know nothing about the identity of these editors, but one thing is clear: their editorial work is nothing short of brilliant. The rapid, unexpected shifts between voices and moods, much like the abrupt transitions between sites, scents, and images, are not the result of sloppy editing but rather part of an underlying notion that the ultimate song of love must convey in its form something of the baffling, dreamlike qualities of amorous pursuits.[9] Love in the Song is too powerful, even explosive, an emotion to be contained within clear boundaries. Words, like kisses, are drenched in wine. If there is any logic, it is an associative dream logic.

When dealing with an ancient text that is the product of collective creativity fostered over many centuries, it is surely impossible to draw a line between the anonymous composers and the nameless editors of the Song. But together, through an untraceable cumulative process involving many hands and many hearts, they invented a language of love that has become a precious touchstone for all time.

The Question of Canonization

The primary enigma of the story of the Song's life is: Why was a daringly sensual poem of love with no reference whatsoever to God or national history included in the Bible? Not only is the context of the Song's composition and editing unknown, but much of the history of its canonization remains obscure. There was apparently a rabbinic dispute regarding the canonicity of the Song. The account of this dispute, however, is sparse and does not spell out the official criteria used to determine canonicity. The one remnant of this debate is Rabbi Akiva's (50–c. 135 CE) memorable declaration that the "whole world is not worth the day on which the Song of Songs was given to Israel for all the Writings are holy and the Song of Songs is the Holy of Holies" (Mishnah Yadayim 3.5). In a striking rhetorical move, Rabbi Akiva, one of the founding sages of rabbinic Judaism, draws on the superlative structure of the phrase "Song of Songs" (*shir ha-shirim*) to turn the text whose holiness was called into question into none other than the "Holy of Holies" (*kodesh kodashim*).

Rabbi Akiva's success in securing the canonical position of the Song has often been attributed to his endorsement of the allegorical reading, a reading by which the ancient love poem is to be regarded as an amorous dialogue between God and the Community of Israel. This argument too easily glosses over the unconventional aspects of the Song's canonization. One may well wonder why the rabbis bothered to reinterpret it as an allegory in the first place. The decision to include the Song in the canon, as some scholars suggest, may have served as compensation for a lacuna in the biblical text: the lack of *eros* in the heavenly spheres.[10] The prophetic metaphor by which God is imagined as husband and the nation as wife does indeed provide a monotheistic modification of polytheistic paradigms of divine *eros*, but the prophets—be they Hosea, Jeremiah, or Ezekiel—are mostly preoccupied with the sinful conduct of the wanton Jerusalem and offer only brief representations of blissful marital moments. The Song, by contrast, revolves around an admirable and extended dialogue of love, which could be used to reinforce those rare uplifting aspects of the prophetic metaphor.

Canon formation, however, is by no means solely a unifying process that eliminates or smoothes over contradictions. Whether consciously or not, whether willingly or despite themselves, the canon-makers included, at times, deviant traditions within the biblical corpus. Alongside the Song of Songs, there are other distinct anomalies in the biblical text, among them books such as Ecclesiastes and Job, whose inclusion in the canon is surely a cause for wonder. What seems to have contributed to the tipping of the scales in favor of these anomalous texts is their tremendous literary power. That the canon-makers wouldn't have used such terms to justify their choices doesn't make aesthetic considerations less pertinent.

Not just any love song could have been canonized. The admiration for the Song, we may surmise, was so singularly great that it couldn't but be included in the cherished corpus of the community. Some indication of the Song's privileged position is evident in Rabbi Akiva's attempt to set limits on its circulation in nonreligious contexts. "He who trills his voice in chanting the Song of Songs in the banquet house and treats it as a sort of song," Rabbi Akiva announces, "has no part in the world to come" (Tosefta Sanhedrin 12:5). If the

Song hadn't been so popular, there would have been no reason for this warning.

In addition to the Song's textual charm, its musical adaptations may have added to its glamor: it was, after all, sung, according to Rabbi Akiva's account. In biblical Hebrew there is no distinction between song and recited poem: *shir* or *shira* may refer to both. What is more, there are indications in the Song itself that some of the amorous exchanges were intended to be sung, possibly at a feast: "You who dwell in the garden, / friends listen for your voice. / Let me hear it" (8:13). To be sure, there is no record of those ancient melodies, but the rich history of the musical reception of the Song amply illustrates the musicality of the text.

The phenomenon of popular songs and melodies finding their way into religious practice, though not intended for such circulation by their authors or composers, is well known from later contexts. Thus Martin Luther, the towering figure of the German Reformation, used melodies of tavern songs as the musical base for his new liturgy, and Rabbi David Buzaglo, the greatest Moroccan twentieth-century liturgical poet, composed *piyyutim* (liturgical poems) whose tunes were borrowed from the love songs of Egypt's legendary diva Umm Kulthum. Although crossings between the secular and religious spheres are more common in music, this phenomenon is also relevant to poetry. One of the most fascinating contemporary examples is the inclusion of the iconoclastic poems of Yehuda Amichai, poems that were by no means intended for liturgical use, in the prayer books of Reform Jewish congregations.

But what if the Song was intended to be understood allegorically from the very outset? Less probable—but not impossible. Ancient interpreters of the Song may have relied on a grid of codes that are not manifest in the text itself but would have been known to all. Experts of ancient Near East culture in the 1920s went so far as to assume that the Song was a collection of divine poems inspired by the sacred marriage hymns and ceremonies of Mesopotamia. In an attempt to solve the riddle of the Song's canonization, they claimed that the ancient love poem was included in Holy Writ because it served as a monotheistic counterpart to Mesopotamian celebrations of divine love.[11]

Even if we reject the "cultic approach" (as it is called), as most scholars in recent decades have, it still may shed light on the question of the Song's inclusion in the canon. The very fact that there was a genre of divine love poetry in the ancient Near East may have facilitated the transformation of a secular corpus of love poetry into a sacred one.

There is yet another possibility. Perhaps the distinction between earthly and divine love poetry was blurred in the context of the Song's composition, which is why it could circulate in both banquet houses and religious settings until Rabbi Akiva changed the rules of the game. The thriving double life of the Song in medieval Jewish culture in Spain, where verses from the ancient love poem were evoked both in courtly, secular feasts and in liturgical poetry, may shed light on another route altogether.

One can only speculate about the process of the Song's canonization, but it is important to bear in mind that the history of the circulation of texts is replete with surprises. There is no better proof of this than the remarkably lengthy biography of the Song, in which we witness, in each and every exegetical scene, century after century, unexpected uses of this ancient language of love.

Rethinking the Allegorical–Literal Nexus

The Song of Songs is only eight chapters long, and yet, among all biblical texts, it has had one of the most extensive and tumultuous histories of reception from late antiquity to modern times. For many centuries the predominant tendency—in both Jewish and Christian commentaries—was to read the Song as an allegorical poem whose primary objective was to celebrate divine love. A dramatic shift (one of the most dramatic exegetical shifts of all time) took place with the rise of new readings of the Song as an earthly dialogue between human lovers—first in the secular Hebrew love poetry of medieval Spain and then, more extensively, accompanied by a blunt rejection of allegory, within the intellectual framework of eighteenth-century scholarship.

The aim of this biography is to reconsider the trajectory of the Song's exegetical history. Against the tendency to regard the transition from the allegorical to the literal as clear-cut, we will follow the ways in which these two interpretive lines are inextricably intertwined in a whole array of episodes in the text's biography. All of the various experiences of the body—pleasure and pain, even erotic fervor—are part and parcel of many allegorical readings. And, as surprising as it may at first seem, allegory has not disappeared from the modern exegetical scene. New modes of allegorical interpretation of the Song—scholarly, literary, personal, and communal—have emerged with distinct verve in diverse modern settings.

How to define allegory is a big question. The origins of the term "allegory" are Greek: *allos* (other) and *agoreuein* (to speak in public), in the sense of "other-speaking." It is both a mode of composition and a mode of reading. To compose an allegory usually means to write with a double meaning: a surface meaning and an underlying hidden significance. Allegorical interpretations (*allegoresis*) traditionally entail an explication of such an encoded "other" sense in quest of the higher spiritual facets of a given work. They are not necessarily limited to texts that were written in an allegorical mode. The definition of what counts as allegorical "other-speaking," however, changes significantly as we move from Jewish exegetes to Christian ones, much as it changes over time.

By contrast, the literal meaning of a scriptural book is often regarded as its "plain" sense, closer to the letter, to the grammatical features of the text, innocent of figurative elaborations. But literalism is far from being plain or obvious. As we shall see, there are as many shades of literal readings of the Song as there are allegorical commentaries. What counts as literal in mystical commentaries is entirely different from what is accepted as such by Enlightenment thinkers or feminist critics.

The following three chapters look at pivotal moments in the history of the allegorical exegesis of the Song. Chapter 1, "The Rise of Allegory," explores foundational Jewish and Christian allegories of the Song in late antiquity, primarily the rabbinic (midrashic) corpus of *Song of Songs Rabba* and Origen's *Commentary*. Though the Christian–Jewish dialogue is tense at times, it also reveals a fruitful cross-cultural borrowing and a shared belief that allegory is the most fitting way of reading the biblical love poem. Chapter 2, "Poets and Kabbalists," revolves around two major exegetical innovations of medieval Jewish culture in Iberia: the formidable love poetry of Shmuel HaNagid, Yehuda HaLevi, and Ibn Gabirol and the commentaries of the Zohar, the pinnacle of Jewish mysticism. Chapter 3, "Monastic Loves," opens in medieval France with Saint Bernard of Clairvaux's mystical sermons on the Song and moves on to sixteenth-century Spain to introduce the first woman who ventured to record her meditations on the Song: Santa Teresa of Ávila. While exploring the changing definitions of allegory, we will also explore the fluctuating perceptions of the inter-relations of human and divine love and the growing emphasis on the body and the literal in later allegorical commentaries, both Jewish and Christian.

The final chapters look at modern scenes of reception. Chapter 4, "Modern Scholars and the Quest for the Literal Song," shifts to the radical endorsement of literalism that has persisted from the Enlightenment until today. It focuses on the intriguing role of modern scholars—as different as J. G. Herder, Robert Alter, and Phyllis Trible—in shaping the literal turn in the Song's biography. Though modern scholarship has primarily contributed to the literalist exegetical line, we will trace various allegorical moments within this thriving exegetical realm, from the cultic approach of T. J. Meek to the postmodernist reading of Julia Kristeva. Chapter 5, "The Song of America," considers the Songs of some of America's greatest literary exegetes—Walt Whitman, Herman Melville, and Toni Morrison—highlighting their insistence on interweaving literal and allegorical readings of the ancient love poem. The bulk of the chapter is devoted to Toni Morrison's *Song of Solomon* and *Beloved*, taking into account the privileged position of the Song in African American culture. The Song turns out to be instrumental not only in the shaping of premodern communities but also in defining communal bonds, or transforming communal identities, in diverse modern contexts.

Coming from literature as I do, I highlight in each chapter the changing responses to the specific forms and textures of the Song's language of love and, above all, to its plethora of metaphors. Insofar as allegory is an extended metaphor, the Song's figuration lends itself to allegorical interpretation. But allegorization—both traditional and modern—by no means precludes the literal. I would go so far as to suggest that if the literal and the allegorical are intertwined in commentaries on the Song, it is in part a response to the distinct blurring of boundaries between the literal and the figurative in the ancient love poem itself.

No interpreter of the Song, as we shall see, can remain indifferent to its wonders. If this ancient love poem has a biography, a life, it is because scores of readers have embraced it with unparalleled passion. The opening scene in the long story of the Song's life—its puzzling inclusion in the canon—is a prelude to much that lies ahead. Rabbi Akiva does not merely insist dryly that the Song needs to be canonized but rather claims, with much fervor, that the "whole world is not worth the day on which the Song of Songs was given." Another dictum attributed to Rabbi Akiva spells out the radical quality of his proclamation: "Had the Torah not been given, the world could have been conducted by the Song of Songs" (*Song of Songs Zuta* 1:1). Modern readers are no less passionate. Even those who have no interest whatsoever in searching for sanctity in the Song regard the poem's exquisitely profound exploration of human love and bold celebration of the human body as absolutely vital to their lives. For all readers of the Song—whether modern or premodern—the ancient love poem offers much more than a springboard to reflect on love. It entails an urgent invitation to explore the unformulated reaches of amorous pursuits. It touches on our inescapable fears and anxieties in the realm of love while luring us to plunge in, to experience more fully an emotional intensity that could become our own. If you haven't yet fallen in love with the Song, I can only hope that this biography will draw you into the circle of its lovers.

The Rise of Allegory

From Rabbi Akiva to Origen

"Your two breasts are like two fawns." [Song 7:4]
This refers to Moses and Aaron.
Just as a woman's breasts are her glory and her ornament,
so Moses and Aaron are the glory and the ornament of
    Israel.
Just as a woman's breasts are her charm,
so Moses and Aaron are the charm of Israel . . .
Just as a woman's breasts are full of milk,
so Moses and Aaron are full of Torah.

—*Song of Songs Rabba* 4:5[1]

"Thy name is as perfume poured forth" [Song 1:3].
These words foretell a mystery: even so comes the name
of Jesus to the world, and is "as perfume poured forth"
when it is proclaimed.

—Origen, *First Homily [on the Song of Songs]*[2]

To modern readers, any attempt to regard the Song as
pertinent to sacred history or divine love seems

astonishingly detached from its literal sense. But from the point of view of the rabbis and church fathers of late antiquity, the possibility of interpreting the Song as anything but divine would have been unthinkable: Why else would the Song be included in Scripture if not to serve as a key to the mysteries of the human–divine bond?

To understand readers of late antiquity requires a dive into a different worldview, one in which a woman's breasts, her "charm and glory," could be comparable to the beloved founding figures of Jewish tradition and the lover's desirable name could be analogous to that of Jesus. Our reading of metaphor is culturally bound; it relies on grids of signification that may seem to be organic but are actually determined by convention. Are breasts innately more similar to fawns than to Moses and Aaron? Not really. Similarly, likening the lover's name (rather than body) to perfume requires as surprising a leap of the imagination as does thinking of a divine name as pouring forth fragrance. Allegorists of the Song may seem to us utterly oblivious to the text itself but are in fact well attuned to the exhilarating metaphorical play in the Song. Just as the Song's lovers playfully draw parallels between different semantic fields, so too did early commentators thrive on broadening the horizons of exegetical imagination, seeking unexpected comparisons between earthly and divine loves.

All allegories of the Song rely on the fluidity of love as an emotion that may be experienced in entirely different realms. Love, after all, is not limited to human relations or to a single modality. We love our favorite books ("like" would be too mild a term), a particular tune, the street on which we live, and the ever-changing sounds and scents of the sea. Within the context of the biblical world, the term "love," *ahav*, appears in tales of human love as well as in the momentous commandment to love God: "And you shall love the Lord your God with all your heart and with all your being and with all your might" (Deuteronomy 6:5). Such love for the divine surely differs from interpersonal bonds but is regarded as having the same kind of emotional intensity. That love in the Song is total love, based on absolute commitment—there are no other competing suitors and no other enticing maidens in the vineyards—made it all the more compelling for allegorists. They could easily imagine the lovers of the Song as loving each other "with all their heart and with all their being and with all their might."

In both Jewish and Christian orbits, allegories of the Song flourished in late antiquity, becoming a decisive tool by which Jewish and Christian communities defined themselves. But while the communal allegories of the Song, revolving around the history of either Israel or the Church, prevailed during this period, late antiquity also witnessed the rise of other modes of reading between the lines—mystical exegesis and a more personalistic, Neoplatonic probing of the amorous dramas of the soul. Before we explore the major allegorical commentaries of late antiquity, a few words of background on the intricate history of allegory are called for.

Changing Perspectives on Allegory

Allegorical exegesis is neither a Jewish nor a Christian invention. Allegorical interpretation began in Greek antiquity. Disturbed by the literal meaning of certain representations of the gross behavior of the gods in the works of Homer and Hesiod, Greek philosophers found ways to reinterpret them at variance with their plain sense. Xenophanes, Pythagoras, and Plato, among others, discovered redeeming philosophical truths and illuminating perspectives on wisdom buried under layers of mythological disguise. By late antiquity, Neoplatonic interpreters such as Porphyry and Proclus were providing a more spiritualized reading of mythological texts, treating them as accounts of the progression of the soul through different levels of the cosmos.[3]

It was in the context of late antiquity that Jews and Christians became fervent advocates of allegory. Allegory was endorsed in both Jewish and Christian exegetical milieus and remained a cherished mode of interpretation in both realms for many centuries. The definition of what counts as allegory, however, changes significantly as we move from Jewish exegetes to Christian ones, much as it has changed over time.

But allegory has also had its share of critics. In a Protestant demystification of Catholic interpretive practices,

Luther called allegory a "beautiful harlot who fondles men in such a way that it is impossible for her not to be loved."[4] He himself, however, claimed to have succeeded in escaping the allegorical lure. Allegory became an even greater target of critique in nineteenth-century Romanticism. Goethe and Coleridge, allegory's most adamant opponents, introduced a distinction between the symbol and allegory. While hailing the symbol as intransitive, immediately intuitable, existing in and for itself as well as for what it signifies, they downgraded allegory as a mechanical empty shell, an arbitrary container of unrelated content.[5]

In the twentieth century, however, the Romantic preference was inverted. Walter Benjamin called for an appreciation of allegory as the mode that best represents the complications of signification and viewed the symbol as an illusion of organic wholeness between words and things.[6] In Benjamin's wake, allegory's "other-speaking" has gained new admirers and has been perceived as reflecting something of the fluctuating, fissured condition of language and the world it explores.

The vast history of allegory is inextricably connected with the exegetical history of the Song. In fact, the Song was often the scriptural turf upon which some of the greatest shifts in allegorical thinking took place. As we explore some of the landmarks in these interrelated histories, we will see that there is nothing mechanical or empty in the most distinguished allegories of the Song. Nor are its literal and literary dimensions effaced, lurking as they do in the background with stubborn vitality.

Rabbinic Allegories of the Song
and the Prophetic Marital Metaphor

In rabbinic literature, *midrash* stands for a genre of biblical exegesis as well as for compilations in which such exegesis was eventually preserved. Midrashic commentaries flourished most dramatically in Palestine under Roman and Byzantine rule during the periods of the Tannaitic sages (70 CE–220 CE) and the Amoraic sages (220–500 CE). The most extensive and prominent compilation of midrashim on the Song is *Song of Songs Rabba* (*Shir Ha-Shirim Rabba*).[7] It was probably edited around the sixth or seventh century CE but includes earlier commentaries going back as far as the Tannaitic period.[8]

Midrashic exegesis of the Song—and this is true of midrashic hermeneutics altogether—provides not an interpretation of the text as a whole, but rather a verse-by-verse commentary. Every verse of the Song (and at times even a fragment of a verse or a single word) is seen as requiring utmost attention, as being vital to the exploration of the amorous relationship between God and the Community of Israel. And given that this midrashic corpus is a composite text, offering a patchwork of diverse sources from distinct periods, we receive a plethora of allegories for each and every verse, attributed to a whole gallery of Tannaitic and Amoraic sages.

The rabbis' primary exegetical move in fashioning allegories of the Song is to follow the prophets. They do not say so explicitly, nor do they provide any introductory framework, but they all take their cue from the prophetic envisioning of the bond between God and the nation as a bond of marital love. The marital metaphor is by no means merely an ornamental feature of prophetic rhetoric. Interpersonal relationships are perceived as a key to a deeper understanding of the human–divine covenant. Each prophet, however, fleshes out this metaphor according to his own take on Israel's history and future events and his own take on marriage.[9] At times, this prophetic love story is elaborated to such an extent that it becomes an allegory. No prophet is as keen on turning the biography of the nation into a vivid tale as Ezekiel:

> As to your birth, on the day of your birth, your navel cord was not cut nor were you washed smooth in water. . . . No eye had pity on you to do even one of these to show mercy to you, but you were flung out into the field in the disgust you caused on the day of your birth. And I passed by you and saw you wallowing in your blood, and I said to you, "In your blood live," and I said to you, "In your blood live." Myriad as the plants of the field I made you, and you grew and came of age and put on the finest jewels. Your breasts were ripe and your hair sprung up, but you were stark

naked. And I passed by you and saw you, and, look, your time was the time for lovemaking. And I spread My skirt over you and covered your nakedness, and vowed to you and entered a covenant with you, said the Master, the LORD, and you became Mine. (Ezekiel 16: 4–8)

Ezekiel imagines Israel/Jerusalem as a woman and traces her birth back to the Exodus. Though Egypt is not evoked directly as the locus of origin, the lowly beginnings of the foundling nation seem to refer to scenes of slavery. God, who passes by and notes the dire circumstances of the nascent nation, adjures her to "live" in her blood, to regard the marks of blood on her body as a source of life. But divine benevolence does not end here. After Israel/Jerusalem becomes a full-grown woman whose time of love, or lovemaking (*'et dodim*), has come, God passes by yet again and enters into a covenant with her. In this rapid succession of events, Ezekiel moves from birth to puberty and from Egypt to Mount Sinai. He envisions the covenant at Sinai as a grand marital bond between God and Israel. Under God's wings, the nation has the great privilege of acquiring unparalleled beauty, renown, and wealth.

There is nothing abstract about the union of God and Israel/Jerusalem in Ezekiel. Double personification is used to draw this marital biography.[10] The personification of the nation in particular is so graphic that it includes a detailed account of her nakedness and body parts—even her breasts. What is more, the key term for love in the Song, *dodim*, appears in Ezekiel in the depiction of the physical ripeness of the bride (*dodim* appears six times in the Song and only three times elsewhere in the Bible, in Ezekiel 16 and 23, as well as Proverbs 7:18). It is precisely these qualities—the unabashed embodiment of God and the nation and the resourceful representation of love against the backdrop of national events—that make the prophetic texts a vital point of departure for allegorical readings of the Song.

But whereas Ezekiel, Hosea, and Jeremiah are primarily eager to give a blow-by-blow account of the fall of Jerusalem, to mourn over the agonizing transformation of the glorious wife into a wanton woman, the rabbinic commentaries on the Song provide an extensive pool of positive renditions of the amorous bond between God and the nation. This unique position is underscored in a beautiful midrash on Song 1:15–16: "In all other songs, either He praises them, or they praise him. . . . Here, they praise him and he praises them. He praises them: 'Behold you are beautiful, my love [*ra 'ayati*] . . . your eyes are doves.' And they praise him: 'Behold, you are beautiful, my beloved [*dodi*], truly lovely'" (*Song of Songs Rabba* 1:1).[11]

The rabbis do not mention the fact that God rarely praises Israel "in all other hymns." Yet their emphasis on the unique dialogic character of love in the Song seems to disclose a desire for a break, albeit a limited one, from the hierarchical character of the prophetic imaginings of love. Not only modern readers cherish the rare egalitarian bent of the Song. It must have been alluring for the rabbis as well, given their reading of the Shulamite as representing a more elevated and appealing role for the Community of Israel.

"My Dove in the Rock's Crevices": Midrashic Disputes

The rabbis, like the prophets, seek to interpret the love story of God and Israel within the context of the foundational events of ancient Israel, but they have no interest in standard historiography. In *Song of Songs Rabba*, the contextualization of the Song plays out within an ahistorical framework. Scripture is perceived as a timeless corpus in which every verse is simultaneous with every other verse, allowing for no distinction between "early" and "late." The rabbis' primary goal, what they regard as the most exciting exegetical task, is to find in each and every verse of the Song of Songs a link to the great scenes of Exodus, a link that will underscore the interconnectedness of all scriptural texts.[12]

A good illustration of the rabbis' allegorical project is the series of midrashim on Song 2:14:

My dove in the rock's crevices,
    in the hollow of the cliff,
show me how you look,
    let me hear your voice,

for your voice is sweet

and your look desirable.

The sages are eager to explore "the hour" in which this verse was first said: Was it first uttered by the Red Sea or on Mount Sinai? The rabbinic disputes over the appropriate contextualization of the Song bear a strange resemblance to the disputes among modern scholars over the dating of the Song (or the dating of any other biblical text, for that matter). But there are, of course, significant differences. No biblical critic would date the Song prior to Solomon's rule. In *Song of Songs Rabba*, by contrast, there is no respect for chronology. Although Solomon reigned in a later age, his grand Song—as far as the rabbis are concerned— could only have emerged in the context of the primary episodes of ancient Israel.

Rabbi Akiva, a founding figure within the rabbinic world and a renowned Tannaitic sage, was not only a great supporter of the Song's canonization but also one of its exegetes. *Song of Songs Rabba* includes several of his commentaries, among them his take on Song 2:14. Perhaps it is no coincidence that of all the sages, Rabbi Akiva exhibits the most pronounced passion for the Song of Songs. Love looms large not only in his exegetical endeavors but also in his life. The story of Rabbi Akiva and his wife, Rachel, is one of the greatest love stories in rabbinic literature, if not the greatest. Rabbi Akiva is said to have been forever indebted to his wife for her devotion and for spurring him on to study. His deep appreciation is so singularly great that when his disciples block her from approaching him after he has just returned from many years of studying away from home, he declares: "Let her alone; whatever is mine and yours is hers" (*sheli ve-shelakhem shela hu*) (Ketubot 62b–63a).[13] Note that his passionate acknowledgment of the worthiness of his wife bears resemblance to his fervent proclamation in support of the Song's sanctity. Much as he defines the day on which the Song was given as analogous to the day on which the Torah was given at Mount Sinai, demanding that the text whose sanctity was debated be regarded as the "Holy of Holies," so too does he demand the unexpected from his disciples: to regard a woman they have dismissed as the noblest of all.

It comes as no surprise that in the dispute regarding the "hour" in which the Song's dove first appeared, Rabbi Akiva opts for Mount Sinai. Already in his proclamation, he associates the Song with Sinai, but here, in deciphering the figure of the dove in the clefts, he spells out his exegetical choices:

> R. Akiva decoded the verse [as referring to] the hour that they stood before Mt. Sinai . . . for they were hidden in the hiding places of Sinai. *Show me your visage* [Song 2:14], as it says, "And all of the people saw the voices" [Exod. 20:15]—*Let me hear your voice* [Song 2:14], this is the voice from before the commandments, for it says "All that you say we will do and we will hear" [Exod. 24:7]—*For your voice is pleasant*

[Song 2:14]; this is the voice after the commandments, as it says, "God has heard the voice of your
speaking; that which you have said is goodly"
[Deut. 5:24]. (*Song of Songs Rabba* 2:14)[14]

Rabbi Akiva uncovers a link between the clefts of the
dove and the rocks of Sinai. His exegetical flare, however, is most spectacular in his association of the intoxicating mixture of the senses in the Song with the memorable depiction of the people "seeing the voices" (*ro'im et
ha-kolot*) in Exodus 20:14. The lover's inseparable cravings to both see the beloved's visage and hear her pleas-
ant voice are thus seen as inextricably connected to the
collapse of distinctions between voices and sights in the
monumental revelation scene of Mount Sinai.[15] Though
Rabbi Akiva does not mention Ezekiel 16 explicitly, his
allegorical reading of the Song is undoubtedly inspired
by Ezekiel's perception of Sinai as the most climactic
moment in the love story of God and the nation.

Rabbi Akiva's commentary on the dove scene is not
accepted by all. Alongside commentators who read the
Song's dove against the backdrop of Mount Sinai,
there are others who set it in the context of another
pivotal moment in Exodus: the crossing of the Red
Sea. Rabbi Ishmael's disciple is among them:

The one of the house of R. Ishmael teaches: In the
hour in which Israel went out from Egypt, to what
were they similar? To a dove which ran away from a
hawk, and entered the cleft of a rock and found there
a nestling snake. She entered within, but could not go

in, because of the snake; she could not go back, because of the hawk which was waiting outside. What did the dove do? She began to cry out and beat her wings, in order that the owner of the dovecote would hear and come save her. That is how Israel appeared at the sea. They could not go down into the sea, for the sea had not yet been split for them. They could not go back, for Pharaoh was coming near. What did they do? "They were mightily afraid, and the children of Israel cried unto the Lord" [Exodus 14:10], and immediately "The Lord saved them on that day [Exodus 14:30]. (*Song of Songs Rabba* 2:14)[16]

Rabbi Ishmael's disciple positions the dove in an incredibly specific scene: just before the parting of the Red Sea. Fleshing out the details of the metaphor, he suggests that the dove in the cleft of the rock is desperately trying to avoid two predators: a hawk and a snake. The Israelites' conduct at the shore of the Red Sea is colored by similar anxieties: they fear the sea as much as they fear the approaching Pharaoh. And they would not have come out of their hiding place if God had not lured them with words of love—"My dove."

No decoding in the Midrash is treated as the one and only possible elucidation. To take part in the midrashic exegetical game means to take pleasure in the ever-growing proliferation of interpretive possibilities.[17] Even the exact moment at which the dove of Song 2:14 hid by the Red Sea may be part of a playfully serious dispute.

Rabbi Eliezer too identifies the Red Sea as the most pertinent context for the Song's dove, but for a different reason:

> R. Eliezer decoded [*patar*] the verse [as referring to] the hour that Israel stood at the sea. *My dove in the cleft of the rock in the hiding place of the steep* [Song 2:14], that they were hidden in the hiding place of the sea—*Show me your visage* [Song 2:14]; this is what is written. "Stand forth and see the salvation of the Lord" [Exod. 14:13]—Let me hear your voice; this is the singing, as it says, "Then Moses sang" [Exod. 15:1]—*For your voice is lovely* [Song 2:14]; this is the Song—*And your visage is beautiful* [Song 2:14]; for Israel were pointing with their fingers and saying "This is my God and I will beautify Him" [Song of the Sea, Exod. 15:2]. (*Song of Songs Rabba* 2:14)[18]

Rather than singling out the moment before the crossing, Rabbi Eliezer highlights the crossing itself. Much as the lover calls upon his dovelike beloved to come out of her hiding place and show her beautiful face in a flirtatious hide-and-seek, so too is God revealed in all his glory as the waters part. The exegetical link is validated by the recurrence of the root *r 'ah*, "to see," in both Exodus and the Song.[19] But above all, there is an underlying poetic connection between the two episodes. Rabbi Eliezer is drawn to the Red Sea by the immense poetic power of the Song of the Sea.[20] The passion of that song, which bursts forth at the sight of God's deliverance of his people in Exodus 15, is seen as akin to the passion evident in the Song of Songs when the lover revels in his beloved's desirable look.

Interestingly, gender consistency is not a concern in these midrashim. According to the overriding allegorical grid, the lover represents God and the beloved stands for the Community of Israel, but for both Rabbi Eliezer and Rabbi Akiva, the quest to glimpse the Shulamite's visage becomes analogous to the yearning to see God. And yet midrashic fluidity is such that when speaking of the beloved's voice, these two sages associate it with the people's voice. Rabbi Akiva's commentary is even more erratic: he attributes the beloved's voice both to God and to the people.

The Chariot, the Orchard, and the Measure of the Divine Body: Early Mysticism

Within the multifaceted midrashic corpus of *Song of Songs Rabba*, one can also find traces of mystical readings of the Song. The Song would become the most cherished biblical text of Jewish mysticism in the Middle Ages, but it already played a noticeable role in the rabbinic mystical commentaries of late antiquity. Mystical exegetes seek an inner experiential knowledge of God; they crave to decipher ineffable divine mysteries while approaching celestial spheres. What forms the essence of such experiences and how it may be depicted is a great enigma that the mystics themselves are incapable of laying bare fully—or perhaps are reluctant to do so.[21] The midrashim of *Song of Songs Rabba* that record mystical experiences intimate that the most promising way to approach the highest spheres is to yoke verses of the Song to Ezekiel's divine chariot (Ezekiel 1). More specifically, they combine the Song's language of love with practices of *Merkavah* (chariot) mysticism, a particular type of ecstatic contemplation based on Ezekiel's vision of God's glorious throne as a heavenly chariot.[22]

The exchange between Rabbi Akiva and Ben Azzai on the depiction of the beloved's neck as adorned with beads in Song 1:10 touches on the great lure and danger of engaging in chariot mysticism:

> "Your neck with beads" [Song 1:10] ... Ben Azzai was sitting and interpreting [making midrash], and fire was all around him. They went and told Rabbi Akiva, "Rabbi, Ben-Azzai is sitting and interpreting, and fire is burning all around him." He went to him and said to him, "I heard that you were interpreting, and the fire burning all around you." He said, "Indeed." He said, "Perhaps you were engaged in the inner-rooms of the chariot?" He said, "No. I was sitting and stringing the words of Torah [to each other], and the Torah to the Prophets and the Prophets to the Writings, and the words were as radiant as when they were given from Sinai, and they were as sweet as at their original giving. Were they not originally given in fire, as it is written, 'And the

mountain was burning with fire' [Deut. 4:11]?" (*Song of Songs Rabba* 1:10)[23]

Hearing that fire surrounded Ben Azzai while he was expounding, Rabbi Akiva suspects that his companion has engaged in the perilous exegetical practices of chariot mysticism. Linking Ezekiel's chariot and the royal chambers of Song 1:4—"The king has brought me to his chambers (*hadarav*)"—Rabbi Akiva asks: "Perhaps you were engaged in the inner-rooms of the chariot (*hadrei merkava*)"? Ben Azzai, however, admits nothing of the sort. He dissociates himself from esoteric practices by citing another verse from the Song, the focal point of this midrash: Song 1:10. The lovely beads on the beloved's neck allow Ben Azzai to depict his interpretive strategy as that of stringing beads—tying together the words of the Torah, the Prophets, and the Writings. Rather than probing forbidden realms, Ben Azzai assures Rabbi Akiva, he was merely following the traditional midrashic practice of treating all parts of Scripture as if they are inextricably connected: in this case, reading a verse from the Song in light of a verse from the Torah.

But is Ben Azzai teasing Rabbi Akiva? He seems to intimate that (more specifically) he is following in the footsteps of none other than Rabbi Akiva himself. Much as Rabbi Akiva has ventured to link the Song to the sacred events of Mount Sinai, so too does Ben Azzai hint that he has been prompted to use the Song in order to rekindle the fire of the holy mountain, to re-experience the fervent passion of that grand moment in sacred history.

Rabbi Akiva holds a unique position of being both at the heart of the rabbinic establishment and a leading figure of esoteric learning on the margins. His inquisitive visit to Ben Azzai is meant not to eradicate esoteric practices but rather to call for caution. Intense spiritual experiences are what mystics strive for, but rekindling such esoteric fire requires the kind of knowledge that only the select few can acquire.

The rabbinic ambivalence toward Ben Azzai's choices is not limited to his exegetical preferences. Ben Azzai apparently never married (or, according to another account, he married Rabbi Akiva's daughter but deserted her soon after). He chose, instead, an ascetic way of life in which the only cherished love was the love of Torah and God. Asceticism was not encouraged in Jewish circles either in late antiquity or later on: being part of the world, having a family, was regarded as an indispensable component of one's life. Rabbi Akiva's great capacity for human love seems to be among the features of his biography that make him more suitable than the ascetic Ben Azzai for unique mystical experiences.[24]

The midrashic tale about the four who entered the *pardes*, the orchard, sheds further light on the distinction between Rabbi Akiva and Ben Azzai as it probes the hidden meanings of the verse "The king has brought me into his chambers" (Song 1:4):

Four entered [the *pardes*]: Ben Azzai and Ben Zoma, Elisha b. Abuyah and R. Akiva. Ben Azzai gazed and was afflicted.... Ben Zoma gazed and died.... Elisha Ben-Abuya made cuttings among the plantings [that is, became an apostate].... R. Akiva went in whole and came out whole. And he said, "It is not because I am greater than my companions, but this have sages taught in the Mishnah: "Your deeds will draw you near, or your deeds will put you out." ... And in this regard it is said in Scripture, "The king has brought me into his chambers." (*Song of Songs Rabba* 1:4)[25]

The exact meaning of the term *pardes* in this passage has long been an object of speculation. In later interpretations, especially in the Zohar, *pardes* becomes an acronym for the four levels of interpretation (literal, midrashic, philosophical, and mystical). In this midrash from *Song of Songs Rabba*, however, the term *pardes* primarily designates an esoteric realm of exegesis and is construed as synonymous with the royal chambers of Song 1:4. The spatial fluidity of the Song, which allows the lovers to move at the pace of a dream between the inner chambers of the palace and the gardens or orchards of love, between figurative settings and literal ones, is thus translated into allegorical terms in *Song of Songs Rabba*: the chambers and the orchard merge with each other as interrelated esoteric sites of divine love.[26]

Ben Azzai, we discover, is not among those who are fit to endure advanced esoteric experiences. The only one who has the privilege of engaging in mystical exegesis without hazard, the only one who has the privilege of experiencing a singularly intimate contact with the divine king, is Rabbi Akiva. Rabbi Akiva (not the Community of Israel) is cast here in the role of God's beloved. As such, he is deemed worthy of being drawn into and out of the orchard or divine chambers. The sages' choice to evoke the royal chambers of Song 1:4 is not without significance. This verse, as we have seen, is charged with mystical connotations and associated with chariot mysticism. Rabbi Akiva may claim to be no greater than his companions, but his "deeds" turn out to be the true chariot by which he is carried up to the supernal realms of the divine chambers.

We have noted the fragments of esoteric readings embedded in *Song of Songs Rabba*, but the most elaborate Jewish mystical reading of the Song in late antiquity is found in a short, cryptic text titled *Shi'ur Koma* (literally, "the measure of the body," that is, the divine body), presumably dating back to the second or third century CE. *Shi'ur Koma* uses the Shulamite's laudatory, detailed portrayal of the resplendent body of her lover— "My lover is shining white and ruddy. . . . His head is purest gold" (Song 5:10–15)—as a takeoff lane for an exploration of Ezekiel's vision of the divine body (a "figure similar to a man," Ezekiel 1:26) on the celestial throne.[27] Rabbi Akiva is regarded as one of the privileged witnesses of the bodily features of the divine glory.[28]

Jewish commentators of late antiquity were absorbed in endless disputes over the appropriate reading of every verse in the Song. But whether in search of the moment when the beloved dove first appeared or in search of God's esoteric chambers, no rabbi would have argued with the fact that the Song's language of love is the royal road one must travel to unlock the grand riddle of the human–divine bond.

Origen's *Commentary*: Christian–Jewish Dialogue

Christian exegetes in late antiquity were as obsessed with the Song as were the rabbis. The extent to which these communities were familiar with each other's exegetical endeavors remains an unresolved question. But given that Jews and Christians in Roman Palestine of the second and third centuries CE often lived side by side, it is highly plausible that they engaged in dialogue, responding to each other's interpretive practices, even if their writings rarely mention it openly.[29]

Origen, the renowned church father and founding figure of Christian exegesis of the Song, arrived in Caesarea in 230 after being expelled from Alexandria (Demetrius, the bishop of Alexandria, had apparently accused the young theologian of being disrespectful).[30] Caesarea at that time was a bustling port and the administrative center of the Roman province of Judaea, with a diverse population of pagans, Jews, and Christians. We do not have detailed records of

Origen's interactions with the Jewish community of Caesarea, but in *Contra Celsum* Origen mentions his disputes with Jewish learned men over the proper decoding of scriptural truths. Some of these debates may have been over the right interpretation of the Song and could have taken place in Caesarea's *odeum*, meeting place, where religious debates were held.[31]

Origen wrote his ten-volume *Commentary* on the Song in the years 245–247 CE, initially during a visit to Athens and then in Caesarea.[32] Most of the original Greek of Origen's *Commentary* has been lost, but four books were translated into Latin by Rufinus (providing explications only until the "little foxes" of 2:15!), and two of his homilies were translated by Jerome. Jerome beautifully defines Origen's great accomplishment in his introductory remarks: "While Origen surpassed all writers in his other books, in his *Song of Songs* he surpassed himself. . . . And this exposition of his is so splendid and so clear, that it seems to me that the words, *The King brought me into His chambers*, have found their fulfillment in him."[33] If in *Song of Songs Rabba* Rabbi Akiva is cherished as the one who entered the inscrutable chambers of the divine king, within the Christian world Origen is extolled as the "fulfillment" of this verse.

In the first section of Origen's Prologue to his *Commentary*, he acknowledges his debt to rabbinic practices in recommending that "everyone who is not yet rid of the vexations of flesh and blood" should refrain from reading the Song of Songs:

For they say that with the Hebrews also care is taken to allow no one even to hold this book in his hands, who had not reached a full and ripe age. And there is another practice too that we have received from them—namely, that all the Scriptures should be delivered to boys by teachers and wise men, while at the same time the four that they call *deuteröseis*—that is to say, the beginning of Genesis, in which the creation of the world is described; the first chapters of Ezekiel, which tell about the cherubim [of the Chariot] . . . and this book of the Song of Songs—should be reserved for study till the last.[34]

Origen seems to be referring here to the rabbis' cautious approach to the blending of the Song and Ezekiel in chariot mysticism and *Shi'ur Koma*. Interestingly enough, this passage provides the most detailed surviving account of the rabbinic instructions regarding the study of the Song.[35]

In the following sections of Origen's Prologue, he doesn't speak openly of the rabbinic exegetical sphere, but his readings of the Song include implicit references to the teachings of contemporary Jewish commentators. This Christian–Jewish dialogue is by no means innocent of polemical intentions. Origen relies on Jewish allegories and their use of the prophetic marital metaphor but is determined to fashion a distinctly Christian allegorical framework that will offer both a new historical perspective on the Song and a new mystical outlook. Consider Origen's comments on the superlative title of the Song of Songs in the fourth section of the Prologue:

> We must now pass on to our next point, and discuss the actual title of "The Song of Songs." You find a similar phrase in what were called *the holies of holies . . .* and again in the *works of works* mentioned in the Book of Numbers, and in what Paul calls *the ages of ages. . . .*
>
> But we must enquire for the first time what are the songs in relation to which this song is called "The Song of Songs." I think they are the songs that were sung of old by prophets or by angels. For the Law is said to have been *ordained by angels in the hand of the mediator*. All those, then, that were uttered by them, were the introductory songs sung by the Bridegroom's friends; but this unique song is that which the Bridegroom Himself was to sing as His marriage-hymn, when about to take His Bride; in which same song the Bride no longer wants the Bridegroom's friends to sing to her, but longs to hear her Spouse who now is with her, speak with His own lips; wherefore she says: *Let Him kiss me with the kisses of His mouth.*
>
> Rightly, then, is this song preferred before all songs. The other songs that the Law and the prophets sang, were sung to the Bride while she was still a little child and had not yet attained maturity. But this song is sung to her, now that she is grown up, and very strong, and ready for a husband's power and the

perfect mystery. It is said of her for this reason: *My perfect dove is but one.* (46–47)

Origen's association of the Song's title with the phrase "holy of holies" calls to mind Rabbi Akiva's endorsement of the Song's sanctity. But the church father does not stop there. But the church father does not stop there. He moves from the Old Testament's "holies of holies" (Exodus 30:29) and "work of works" (Numbers 4:47) to Paul's "ages of ages," indicating from the outset that any reading of the Old Testament must ultimately lead to a meditation on the eternal glory of Christ.

In Origen's allegorical world, the Song is an epithalamium, a nuptial song, whose protagonists are Christ as Bridegroom and the Church as Bride. This glorious wedding is the culmination of a historical tale. In the days of the Old Testament, the Synagogue was the Bride. Immature as the Synagogue was, she could only yearn for Christ, but this yearning was not satisfied.[36] The Synagogue's only companions were the friends of the Bridegroom—the angels and the prophets—who sang to her as intermediaries. But once the Bride attained maturity and became the Church, the gates of heavenly love and heavenly singing opened before her. The Bridegroom kissed her with the kisses of his own lips (with no mediation whatsoever) and addressed her with a song of love: "My perfect dove is but one." No other song, as far as Origen is concerned, could come close to the poetic perfection of this nuptial celebration of perfect love.[37] True, there were other songs that were sung by the prophets and angels (he later lists some of them meticulously, from the Song of the Sea to David's song in the Book of Kings, Isaiah's vineyard song, and Psalms), but, for all their grandeur, they were merely "introductory songs," which pale in comparison with the one song the Bridegroom himself sang as a "marriage-hymn."

Against the midrashic use of the Song to highlight the singular position of the Community of Israel as the only nation worthy of an amorous relationship with God, Origen adopts the Pauline line according to which Christ's revelation supersedes the revelation at Sinai. What makes the Song of Songs synonymous with the Holy of Holies in his *Commentary* is not the fire of Mount Sinai but rather the coming of Christ and the emergence of the Church as the chosen Bride.

In constructing his *Commentary*, Origen relies on a whole range of scriptural texts. As in Jewish exegesis, seeking connections between different biblical texts is a major strategy of Christian exegesis, though the contours of this enterprise are different. Unlike the rabbinic exegetes, the church father juggles citations from both the Old Testament and the New Testament. We have noted Origen's use of Paul's "age of ages," but he also alludes to Galatians 3:19—"Wherefore then serveth the law? It was added because of transgressions, till the seed should come to whom the promise was made; and it was ordained by angels in the hand of a mediator"—in positioning Christ's Song as superior to the songs offered by the Mosaic Law. The exegetical goal of the *Commentary* is not quite to string together the Torah, the Prophets, and the Writings as linked beads but rather to search for prefigurations of the New Testament in the Old Testament that can underscore the primacy of Christian faith.

Amorous Dramas: Between the Yearning Church and the Yearning Soul

Well attuned to the performative features of the Song, Origen defines the nuptial Song as "written in the form of a drama" (21). With dramatic sensibility and an unmistakable familiarity with Neoplatonic allegories, he stages the different sequences in the ancient love poem as vivid scenes in a spiritual play. Thus, in the more elaborate commentary on the Shulamite's opening words, the Bride is depicted as she appears "on the stage, having received for her betrothal and by way of dowry most fitting gifts from a most noble bridegroom; but, because the bridegroom delays in his coming for so long, she, grieved with longing for his love, is pining at home and doing all she can to bring herself at last to see her spouse, and to enjoy his kisses" (58–59). To understand the "inner meaning" of this scene, Origen explains, one needs to picture her as "the Church who longs for union with Christ" (59).

The Bride, however, is not only a "corporate personality" representing the Church but also the individual soul burning with celestial love: "The appellations of

Bride and Bridegroom denote either the Church in her relation to Christ or the soul in her union with the Word of God" (58). Put differently, Origen provides both a historical allegory and a tropological Neoplatonic reading that focuses on the soul.[38] From the scene of the longing Church, Origen shifts to the more mystical drama of the soul, "whose only desire is to be united to the Word of God . . . and to enter into the mysteries of His wisdom and knowledge as into the chambers of her heavenly Bridegroom" (60). The soul's craving to be kissed turns out to be a craving to be enlightened by the visitation of the Word of God, the Logos, to be filled "with divine perception and understanding without the agency of human or angelic ministration" (61). It is a mystical-hermeneutic desire to be capable of discerning the obscure parables and riddles of the Word. Origen probes the linguistic details of the verse and interprets the plural form of "kisses" (the Shulamite could have, after all, asked just for one kiss) as a purposeful comment on exegetical pleasures: "The plural, 'kisses,' is used in order that we may understand that the lighting up of every obscure meaning is a kiss of the Word of God bestowed on the perfected soul" (61).

Throughout his commentaries, Origen oscillates between the dramas of the Church-Christ and the Soul-Logos. His meditation on the courting scene of Song 2, in which the lover lures his dovelike beloved to come out of the cleft, is another notable example. This dove that so intrigues the rabbis becomes an entirely different bird-Bride in Origen's hands:

> In the sequence of the drama before us, the Bride-
> groom who has come to His Bride leaping upon the
> mountains and springing forth upon the hills says . . . :
> "Arise, come, my neighbor, my fair one, my dove." . . .
> After this, speaking as though the Bride were veiled
> and covered for the sake of reverence, the Bridegroom
> asks her . . . to lay aside her veil and show her face
> to Him. (246–247)

The Bride's face and voice are not unknown to the
Bridegroom, Origen points out, which is why the invitation to step out and leave the veil behind indicates a
call for transformation.

Here too a drama of the soul is set into motion. The
Bridegroom's plea is a wakeup call, delivered to a soul
that is trapped in a stagnant state of winter. As long as
the soul is "battered by the storms of her vices and the
strong blasts of malignant spirits" (247–248), she is
unable to "smell" the flowers of the Divine Scriptures
and fathom their deeper wisdom. But when the winter
has passed, the Word of God comes to her and "calls
her to Himself, and bids her come forth" (248).

For Origen, the rock where the dove hides is none
other than the rock of Christ from 1 Corinthians 10:4:
"For they drank from the spiritual rock that accompanied them, and that rock was Christ." Thus, he concludes, "And here, then, under the cover of the rock,
the Word of God invites the soul that has been made
His neighbor, to this place . . . to contemplate things
that are eternal and unseen" (250). It is a scene of

teaching, whereby the soul gradually relinquishes "bodily concerns and physical perceptions," gaining insight into "the mysteries of the age to come" (252).

Rightly defined as a Christian Platonist, Origen makes ample use of Platonic idiom in constructing his allegorical framework. The soul's emergence as a dove from the cleft becomes a Christological version of Plato's allegory of the cave. That Plato too uses allegory as a heuristic tool makes his renowned cave all the more enticing. In Origen's spiritual drama, the soul initially appears in a state of blindness, analogous to that of the prisoners in Plato's cave, who see shadows and mistakenly view them as the sole reality. But then, like the one prisoner who manages to escape the cave, the soul/dove discovers what lies beyond this world of shadowy illusions and becomes accustomed to the dazzling light of the sun. This process is not an easy one—either in the *Republic* or in the *Commentary*. Origen's soul, though, is fortunate to have a devoted Bridegroom (something of a grand philosopher) who patiently instructs her until she can emerge out of the state of ignorance, take the veil off her eyes, and contemplate "things that are eternal and unseen."

The Question of the Flesh: Corporeal and Incorporeal Harts

What is the role of the literal within this complex interplay of levels of meaning? Origen is no lover of the flesh. At some point, while Origen was still in Alexandria, he apparently took Matthew 19:12 ("And there be eunuchs, which have made themselves eunuchs for the kingdom of heaven's sake") seriously and castrated himself.[39] This incident is recorded in Eusebius of Caesarea's *Ecclesiastical History*, the primary source of information on Origen's life. According to Eusebius, Origen wanted "both to fulfill the Savior's saying, and also that he might prevent all suspicion of shameful slander on the part of unbelievers (for, young as he was, he used to discourse on divine things with women as well as men)."[40] Whether or not Origen actually castrated himself (some have questioned the validity of Eusebius's report), he was one of the founding figures of Christian asceticism. Asceticism followed an entirely different trajectory in the Christian world. It drew a considerable number of followers in late antiquity and then became even more prominent in medieval monasticism as well as in subsequent monastic trends. As a zealous advocate of the ascetic mode of life, Origen delivers some of the most scathing condemnations of carnal love, among them the following declaration: "[There is] a love of the flesh which comes from Satan, and there is also another love, belonging to the spirit, which has its origin in God; and nobody can be possessed by the two loves. . . . If you have despised all bodily things . . . then you can acquire spiritual love" (270).[41]

The interplay between the corporeal and the incorporeal in Origen's *Commentary*, however, is more complex and deserves closer examination. Origen's commentary on the metaphor of the lover as "a roe or a young hart upon the mountains" (2:9) displays the intricacies of his interpretive theory:

> So, as we said at the beginning, all the things in the visible category can be related to the invisible, the corporeal to the incorporeal, and the manifest to those that are hidden; so that the creation of the world itself, fashioned in this wise as it is, can be understood through the divine wisdom, which from actual things and copies teaches us things unseen by means of those that are seen, and carries us over from earthly things to heavenly. . . .
>
> If, therefore, in accordance with the principles that we have established all things that are open stand in some sort of relation to others that are hidden, it undoubtedly follows that the visible hart and roe mentioned in the Song of Songs are related to some patterns of incorporeal realities, in accordance with the character borne by their bodily nature. And this must be in such wise that we ought to be able to furnish a fitting interpretation of what is said about the Lord perfecting the harts, by reference to those harts that are unseen and hidden. (223)

In this passage Origen draws a comparison between the structure of Scripture and that of the universe. Just as the world is based on a dualist structure of corporeal/visible things correlating to incorporeal/invisible things, so too is Scripture. Visible events—the literal truths of both the Old Testament and the Gospels are not denied—find their true correspondences in the superior "hidden things" of the heavenly spheres. Similarly, the visible harts and roes are part and parcel of a dualism that is vital to any attempt to fashion a "fitting interpretation." Rather than eliminating the physical creatures, Origen insists that "the character borne by their bodily nature" deserves attention and offers an indispensable clue to understanding invisible harts and incorporeal realities.

There is always a Platonic dimension to Origen's conception of the interrelations between the literal and the allegorical. Just as Platonic *eros* can be construed as a striving for the forms of the Good and the Beautiful, so can allegorical exegesis be seen as the attempt of the reader, facing incomplete or thin literal readings, to reach a fuller or deeper meaning.[42] Origen's Song, then, is far from a bodiless text: its harts can display the *real* contours of the letter.

Rabbinic Responses to Origen

Origen's *Commentary* became the touchstone of all Christian allegories in late antiquity. Jerome, who translated some of Origen's homilies, used the *Commentary* as the point of departure for his own reading of the Song. Ambrose followed suit, as did many others. But the reception of Origen's work was not limited to Christian circles. Some of the later

midrashim of *Song of Songs Rabba* may have been polemical responses to Origen's *Commentary*.

One such midrash, attributed to two Amoraic sages
of the fourth century CE, Rabbi Azariah and Rabbi
Judah (son of Rabbi Simon), revolves around the
opening kisses of the Song (one of Origen's favorite
topics):

> R. Azariah and R. Judah b. R. Simon . . . said: "It is
> written, 'Moses commanded us the Torah' [Deut.
> 33:4]. In the entire Torah there are six hundred
> thirteen commandments. The numerical value of the
> letters in the word 'Torah' is only six hundred eleven.
> These are the ones that Moses spoke to us. But 'I [am
> the Lord your God]' and 'You will not have [other
> gods besides me]' [Exod. 20:1–2] we have heard not
> from the mouth of Moses but from the Mouth of the
> Holy One, blessed be He. That is in line with this
> verse: 'O that you would kiss me with the kisses of
> your mouth'" (*Song of Songs Rabba* 1:2)[43]

The two sages wonder why the numerical value of the
sum of the letters of the word "Torah" (each letter of
the Hebrew alphabet has numerical value) is 611,
whereas the number of precepts given at Sinai is 613. In
search of the missing two commandments, they en-
dorse the view that the Israelites heard the first two
commandments directly from God (and not from
Moses): "I am the Lord your God" and "You will not
have other gods besides me" (Exodus 20:1–3). In light
of these intricate calculations, the two sages read the

verse "O that you would kiss me with the kisses of your mouth" as referring to the commandments that were uttered via God's mouth without mediation. Origen's claim that Christianity has been granted direct revelation whereas Judaism relies solely on mediators, they seem to intimate, is utterly false and misleading.[44]

Jewish responses to Origen, however, may also be embedded in midrashim attributed to earlier sages of the third century CE. The following midrash by Rabbi Yohanan, a contemporary of Origen and possibly Origen's most notable Jewish opponent, points to another possibility.[45] According to Rabbi Yohanan's commentary on Song 1:2, an angel carried forth the Ten Commandments to the Israelites at Sinai asking whether they would be willing to accept the authority of the Word. Although the angel provided an unappetizing list of rules and commitments, the Israelites (one by one) did not hesitate to say, "Yes." Each Israelite thus deserves to be kissed by the angel. Rabbi Yohanan emphasizes the presence of the angel as an intermediary to avoid the blunt anthropomorphism of a divine kiss. He may be responding to Origen or vice versa. Or perhaps their paths crossed in Caesarea and they influenced each other.

The Jewish–Christian dialogue concerning the Song in late antiquity is surely tense, but it also reveals a fruitful cross-cultural borrowing and a shared belief that allegory is the true way of reading the biblical love poem. The only question that keeps lingering—not a minor one—is what kind of allegory. In the next two chapters, we will move from rabbinic and early Christian commentaries on the Song in late antiquity to later masterpieces of Jewish and Christian allegorical exegesis from the Middle Ages until the sixteenth century. Some of the exegetical trends of *Song of Songs Rabba* and Origen's *Commentary* reemerge in these later contexts, but, as we shall see, they acquire different forms and different meanings.

Poets and Kabbalists

From Medieval Hebrew Poetry to the Zohar

Long before the Enlightenment, the Song of Songs was cherished as a touchstone of earthly love in the secular Hebrew poetry of medieval Spain. This remarkable corpus of love poetry flies in the face of the common perception that full-blown literal readings of the ancient love poem first emerged in the writings of eighteenth-century scholars and literati. What makes medieval Hebrew poetry all the more fascinating is the fact that love poems saturated with the language and themes of the Song were composed both in the domain of secular poetry (*shirat ha-hol*) and in the realm of liturgical poetry (*shirat ha-kodesh*), circulating simultaneously in worldly courts and in synagogues. No Hebrew poet in medieval Spain would have endorsed Rabbi Akiva's demand to limit the circulation of the Song to the religious sphere and refrain from singing it at banquets.

This formidable scene of the poetic reception of the Song, spanning the tenth to twelfth centuries, was followed by another exegetical pinnacle in the Song's biography when the Zohar appeared onstage in the thirteenth century. In the Zohar, the monumental corpus of Jewish mysticism, the ancient love poem becomes the pivotal text used to define the amorous ties between the *sefirot*, the divine emanations, as well as the flow between the upper and the lower worlds.

These Hebrew poets and the kabbalists who followed them belonged to different worlds. To begin with, the bulk of medieval Hebrew poetry emerged in Muslim Andalusia, or al-Andalus (southern Spain), whereas the Zohar was composed in Castile (northern Spain) against the backdrop of Christian rule. What is more, one can hardly imagine any kabbalist welcoming the kind of literal adaptations of the Song that were so popular in the court culture of medieval Hebrew poets. And yet there are points of affinity. Midrashic commentaries on the Song served as a primary source for both the liturgical poetry of al-Andalus and the Zohar. More surprisingly, even within the spheres of the celestial loves depicted in the Zohar, the literal and sexual dimensions of the Song are underscored in unprecedented ways.

Abraham Ibn Ezra: Changing Perceptions of the Literal Sense

In his commentary on the Song of Songs, Abraham Ibn Ezra (1089–1164) formulates some of the underlying presuppositions of many Hebrew poets in medieval Spain. A renowned biblical commentator and poet as well as a grammarian and philosopher, Ibn Ezra is often extolled as one of the greatest medieval advocates of the *peshat*, the plain sense of Scripture.[1] The literal sense of scriptural texts is never discarded in the Midrash but remains yoked to the allegorical mode of expounding, the *drash*. A significant shift in the status of the literal sense occurred in the Middle Ages as the *peshat* came to be increasingly valued as a vital component of exegesis worthy of being investigated for its own sake.[2] Ibn Ezra's biblical exegesis is exemplary of this new kind of attention to the *peshat*. He presents his literalist approach in a wide range of commentaries on diverse biblical texts from Genesis to Job. His commentary on the Song is particularly intriguing, given that he sets the literal reading of the ancient love poem on the same footing as the allegorical one. To be more specific, Ibn Ezra's commentary on the Song consists of three expositions: the first is grammatical, providing meticulous philological notes on the Song's vocabulary, especially its obscure terms; the second is literal, focusing on the "natural meaning after the Peshat"; and the third is allegorical, construed in accordance with midrashic exegetical principles.[3]

Ibn Ezra's elucidation of the Song's literal sense in his second exposition is the most innovative section of his commentary. He spells out the details of an earthly love between a maiden and a shepherd, reconstructing a plot of sorts. A maiden sees a shepherd passing by in the vineyards one day and falls in love with him.

Longingly, she says in her heart, "O that he would kiss me with repeated kisses!" Then, "as if he were listening to her, she says, For thy love gladdens the heart more than wine."[4] Literal in this case means not only earthly but also literary. Ibn Ezra follows the nuances of the lovers' discourse as he explores the transitions between internal ruminations and imaginary speech.

Metaphors loom large in Ibn Ezra's account of the literary grandeur of the *peshat*, treated in ways that the rabbis of late antiquity would have found unacceptable. Rather than comparing the beloved's breasts to Moses and Aaron, Ibn Ezra reads the lover's metaphor—"Your two breasts are like two fawns"—within its literary, textual context, anticipating the methodologies of modern biblical criticism. Noting that the lover expands the fawn metaphor as he fleshes out a scene of pastoral browsing—"Your two breasts are like two fawns . . . / that graze among the lilies" (Song 4:5)—Ibn Ezra suggests that the two breasts "have sweet fragrance like two fawns which feed among the lilies."[5] Fragrance turns out to be the shared attribute of breasts and fawns. It may seem rather unflattering (though animal scents have their charm), but these particular fawns browse among the lilies and as such exude an exquisite flowery fragrance. With remarkable poetic sensibility, Ibn Ezra not only highlights the immediate textual surroundings of the fawn metaphor but also draws on broader figurative networks in the Song, from the beloved's likening of the lover to a sachet of myrrh between her breasts (Song 1:13) to the recurrent image of the lover as a fawn, gazelle, or stag that at times grazes "among the lilies" (Song 2:16).

Ibn Ezra's literal-literary exposition of the Song is only loosely connected to the allegorical reading that follows. Both expositions are set side by side as different interpretive modes, each valuable in its own right. Other Hebrew poets of medieval Spain did not write commentaries on the Song, but in their insistence on evoking the Song both in their secular love poetry and in their liturgical poems, they exhibit the same kind of freedom that is evident in Ibn Ezra's expositions: the freedom to both savor the *peshat* of the Song and embrace its allegorical potentialities.

The Secular Gazelle of Medieval Hebrew Poetry

The outburst of Hebrew poetry in medieval Spain was inspired by the highly sophisticated modes of Arabic poetry that prevailed in Muslim al-Andalus. Arabic poetry offered a new world of vivacious secular genres—love poetry and wine poetry, as well as mixtures of the two—that had been heretofore unknown in Jewish circles. The giants of medieval Hebrew poetry adopted these genres of Arabic poetry with much flare, molding them to suit their own cultural heritage.[6] Arabic love poetry, in particular, turned out to be vital to their innovative adaptations of the Song.

The origins of medieval Arabic love poetry lie in pre-Islamic times, in Bedouin desert culture and its preoccupation with the desperate loves of nomads. Although Islamic authorities would reject this poetic corpus, it lived on (in modified form) in Muslim al-Andalus. Highly stylized, this poetry relies on stock themes and metaphors. The gazelle, the amorous epithet for the beloved, is among its most renowned figures. The Arabic *ghazăl* may be translated as gazelle, hart, roe, buck, or doe, but it always serves as a stock epithet for the beloved and as a metaphor for her unparalleled beauty.[7] The beloved, then, is more of a type than a specific individual. The objective is not to reduce the unique allure of the loved one, but rather to elevate her as an ideal of beauty.[8]

Unrequited love is a primary concern within this genre. The beloved is often portrayed as strikingly indifferent or hard-hearted, arousing love with her dazzling beauty but never yielding. Another notable feature of Arabic love poetry is its gender fluidity: the gazelle may be either female or male and at times both. Such fluidity adds much to the playful disposition of this poetic corpus.[9]

When the Arabic gazelle crosses into the neighboring fields of medieval Hebrew love poetry (*shirey heshek*), it is reimagined via the vocabulary of the Song of Songs. Alongside their openness to Arabic poetics, medieval Hebrew poets were also proud of their own heritage, eager to tap into the reservoir of Jewish tradition, with its own grand poem of love. What made the Song all the more relevant to their hybrid poetic invention was the fact that the fawn, the gazelle, and the stag are all key metaphors in the ancient love poem, and thus the terms *tzvi* (f. *tzviya*) and *ofer* (f. *ofra*) could be easily fused with the Arabic gazelle.[10] This unique mixture of biblical and Arabic gazelles first appeared in secular love poetry and was then transferred to the liturgical sphere. We will begin with the secular gazelle, the product of the primary cross-cultural exchange between Arabic and Hebrew love poetry.

Shmuel HaNagid (993–1056), one of the greatest poets of this golden age of Hebrew poetry, was also the vizier of Granada's ruler and a leader of the Jewish community. The very archetype of the Andalusian courtier-rabbi, he was the most prominent pioneer of secular Hebrew love poetry. Consider his following poem, "The Gazelle":

The Gazelle

I'd give everything I own for that gazelle
    who, rising at night to his
            harp and flute,
        saw a cup in my hand
        and said:
"Drink your grape blood against my lips!"
    And the moon was cut like a D,
        on a dark robe, written in gold.[11]

Imagine a banquet at which this love poem would have been recited, with charming young boys serving wine to guests who had gathered to savor the beauty of the world and of poetry.[12] Love poetry in medieval al-Andalus was meant not for intimate encounters between individual lovers but rather as a source of amusement and of poetic pleasure in courtly celebrations. Different echoes of the Song intersect in "The Gazelle" against such a courtly backdrop. The theme of wine as comparable with love or intertwined with its tastes is apparent in the opening words of the Shulamite: "Let him kiss me with the kisses of his mouth, / for your loving is better than wine" (1:2). But within the context of Andalusian wine parties, the feast-like episodes of the Song—most notably Song 5:1, "Eat, friends, and drink, / be drunk with loving"—are also set in relief.

Into these metaphorical and literal wine-drinking scenes enters the gazelle. In the Song, the gazelle or the stag mostly meanders in the fields and only once approaches the human sphere by peeping through the windows (Song 2:9). HaNagid's gazelle is more clearly personified and as such discloses an affinity with Arabic love poetry. The link to the Arabic gazelle is all the more noticeable given the homoerotic dimension of the flirtatious exchange between the speaker and the gazelle he'd give anything for. With the touch of bloody wine on the lips—"Drink your grape blood against my lips!"—"The Gazelle" calls to mind a homoerotic love poem by Ibn Shuhaid (992–1035) of Cordoba: "I kissed his throat, / a white jewel / drank the vivid red of his mouth / and so passed the night with him / deliciously until darkness smiled, / showing the white teeth of dawn."[13]

In HaNagid's "In Fact I Love That Fawn" we witness an even more provocative blend of biblical and Arabic gazelles. Rather than an intoxicating gazelle, here the fawn roams about his loved one's garden cutting roses, not unlike the lover in Song 6:2.

In Fact I Love That Fawn

In fact I love that fawn,
>   cutting roses in your garden—
> which is why I've earned your wrath.
>>   If you could see him,
>>   the others would never find you.

"Scrape me some honey
>   from your hive," he said.
"I'll have mine from your tongue,"
I replied. Then he bristled
>   and said to me, sullen:
"And sin before the living God?"
"The sin's on me," I answered, "my lord."[14]

Against the backdrop of the amorous garden of the Song, HaNagid fleshes out one of the most erotic depictions of the beloved's mouth: "Nectar your lips drip, bride, / honey and milk are under your tongue" (Song 4:11). That the fawn is male doesn't stop HaNagid from making a graphic request to receive honey from the lover's tongue. Sin seems to pose no threat to the speaker, who playfully responds to his lover's concern: "The sin's on me."[15] The gender of the gazelle is primarily male, but a woman lurks behind the scenes.

The final exchange calls to mind Abigail's words to David as they scheme together: "And she flung herself at his feet and said, 'Mine, my lord, is the blame!'" (1 Samuel 25:24). Walt Whitman, who unabashedly defies normative definitions of sin as he oscillates between heterosexual and homosexual modes of love in his homage to the Song in "Song of Myself" (a poem we'll discuss in detail in chapter 5), apparently had medieval precursors.

Is it possible that such literal love poems based on the Song flourished in medieval Jewish courts without critique? HaNagid was apparently rebuked for his impropriety—or at least this is what we can infer from a poem in his *Divan* in which he responds to his critics, claiming that his erotic poems need to be read allegorically, much like the Song of Songs: "And its meaning is like that of Solomon's / 'My beloved is radiant' and [her] 'eyes like pools.'"[16] But this apologetic comment may be construed as necessary lip service at the inaugural moment of secular Hebrew love poetry. It doesn't change the fact that HaNagid's secular love poems do not lend themselves to an allegorical reading and were never included in Jewish liturgy. We hear of no critiques regarding the secular love poetry of later medieval Hebrew poets—an absence that serves as a challenge to normative notions of what medieval Jewish culture was like.

Yehuda HaLevi (before 1075–1141), the most famous and revered of the medieval Hebrew poets, was another towering figure of the Jewish community and a courtier. He wrote several short gazelle poems, in this case clearly referring to women.

That Night a Gazelle

That night a gazelle
   of a girl showed me the sun
of her cheek and veil
   of auburn hair,
like ruby over
   a moistened crystal brow,
she looked like dawn's
   fire rising—
reddening clouds with flames.[17]

HaLevi's poem draws on several descriptive sequences in the Song. Combining the portrayal of the beloved in 4:3 ("Like a scarlet thread, your lips . . . / Like cut pomegranate your cheekbones / through the screen of your tresses") with the laudatory description in 6:10 ("Who is this espied like the dawn, / fair as the moon, / dazzling as the sun, / daunting as what looms on high?"), he creates an enticing nocturnal scene in which the gazelle partially reveals herself to the speaker in the dark. Enamored as the speaker is, temporal distinctions utterly collapse. Though the poem is set at night, the encounter with the gazelle prompts him to see the sun on the girl's cheek and a dazzling dawn, "reddening clouds with flame," through her pomegranate-like reddish hair. The Song's sudden dreamy shifts between day and night and excessive metaphorical play—the beloved is likened to a scarlet thread, a pomegranate, the sun, the moon, and the dawn all at once—are endowed with a distinctly new look and distinctly new poetic framework.

There is something daunting and aloof about the gazelle of "That Night a Gazelle," but the hard-heartedness of the Arabic poetic gazelle is far more evident in HaLevi's "A Doe Washes":

A Doe Washes

A doe washes her clothes
    in the stream of my tears
and sets them out to dry
    in the glow of her glory—

she doesn't need the spring's
    water, with my
two eyes, or the sun's
    rays with her splendor.[18]

Here too the trope of the beloved as sun of Song 6:10 appears, but set within a mundane scene of clothes washing by the stream. The stream, we discover, is made of the speaker's desperate tears (the connection is heightened by a pun on the Hebrew term *ayin*, which means both "eye" and "spring"). The doe is so indifferent to the speaker's pain that she can easily wash her clothes in his tears and then dry them out with the glamorous beauty of her sunlike splendor.[19]

The mixtures of biblical and Arabic gazelles/does in medieval secular love poetry acquire different forms as we move from HaNagid to HaLevi, but even within the work of a single poet there are constant shifts in gender, temperament, and tone. The Song's gazelles and laudatory images are invoked in ever-changing ways as different features of Arabic love poetry are translated into the cultural milieu of Jewish courts.

Liturgical Love Poems: Addressing the Divine Lover

The Song's echoes become even more resonant within the realm of liturgical poetry. The secular gazelle travels across her native bounds and reappears, albeit in a different guise, in some of the most renowned liturgical poems of medieval Hebrew poetry. Here indeed allegorical readings of the Song are evident: the evasiveness of the gazelle becomes the emblem of divine absence or anger, and the yearning to see the beloved turns into a quest for the often missing divine lover. The paths of sacred and secular poetry thus intersect, serving as yet another intriguing example of the ways in which the circulation of texts knows no strict borders.

In medieval liturgical love poetry, a midrashic gazelle enters the grove of biblical and Arabic gazelles. *Song of Songs Rabba* offers numerous allegorical gazelles that serve as a point of departure for medieval Hebrew poets in their shaping of allegorical modes of love. In the Midrash, the gazelle (alongside the stag) is primarily an embodiment of the divine lover, and accordingly Song 2:9—"My lover is like a deer / or like a stag" (*domeh dodi le-tsvi o le-ofer ayalim*)—is construed as a depiction of a vigilant, loving God who leaps like a young hart between Egypt, the Red Sea, and Sinai, shielding the Israelites as they wander in the wilderness (*Song of Songs Rabba* 2:9). The liturgical gazelle of medieval poetry has similar attributes, but here the divine *tsvi* has a female counterpart—the *tzviya*, the doe—who stands for the Community of Israel.

Another precursor of this allegorical poetic grove needs to be mentioned: the liturgical poetry, or *piyyut*, of late antiquity. A *piyyut* is a liturgical poem that is sung, chanted, or recited during religious services. This genre took shape in the early Byzantine period with the *piyyutim* of the distinguished poets (*paytanim*) Rabbi Yannai and Rabbi Eleazar Kallir and further developed in the tenth to twelfth centuries in northern Italy and southern Ashkenaz.[20] The Song has a major role in the liturgical poetry composed for Passover (the midrashic association of the Song with the Exodus has its counterparts in the world of the *piyyut*), but it is also a common component of prayers for other holidays—Shavuot and Sukkot—and within the framework of elegiac *piyyutim* commemorating the destruction of the Temple on Tish'a be-Av.[21] Although medieval poets often ridiculed the early *paytanim* for their lack of finesse, they could rely on this early chapter in the history of the poetic reception of the Song as a primary model. In turn, some of the liturgical poems of medieval Hebrew poets transformed the world of *piyyut* and the role of the Song within it. They introduced into Jewish liturgy

FIGURE 1. Marriage ceremony, *Worms Mahzor*, 1272. Illustration accompanying the *piyyut* "Come with me from Lebanon, my bride" (based on Song 4:8). Ms. Heb. 781 = 4, The National Library of Israel, Jerusalem.

both warmth of tone and a sense of immediacy, making room for the poet's inner tumults and yearnings within the framework of communal rituals.

Yehuda HaLevi was not only a master of secular love poetry but also a brilliant composer of liturgical poems. Like other medieval poets, he had a remarkable versatility that allowed him to feel perfectly at home at courtly feasts where earthly pleasures were celebrated as well as in the solemn rituals of the synagogue. His allegorical use of the Song's language of love is most ingenious in poems that address the rift in the amorous bond between God and Israel in times of exile. In "A Doe Far from Home," the "graceful doe so far from her home" recalls precious past scenes when she leaned upon her loving gazelle (*tsvi*) just as the Shulamite leaned upon her lover on coming up from the wilderness (Song 8:5). But those blissful days are long gone, for her divine lover seems to have vanished and her enemies persecute her mercilessly.

The agonies of exilic Israel are further elaborated in HaLevi's "Dove in the Distance," but here the doe is replaced by the Song's dove as a designation of the nation.[22]

A Dove in the Distance

A dove in the distance fluttered,
    flitting through the forest—
      unable to recover
she flew up, flustered, hovering,
    circling round her lover.
      She'd thought the thousand
years to the Time of the End
    about to come, but was
      confounded in her designs,
and tormented by her lover,
    over the years was parted
      from Him, her soul descending
bared to the world below.

> She vowed never again
>   to mention His name, but deep
> within her heart it held,
>   as though a fire burning.
>   Why be like her foes? . . .
>
> and she does not despair,
>   whether she is honored
> through His name or whether
>   in disdain brought low.
> Let God, our Lord, come
>   and not be still: Around Him
>   storms of fire flame.[23]

The opening lines give us a very tangible image of a
dove in flight. The rhythm and profusion of alliterations
of the original Hebrew (*hitofefa-hitnofefa-
chofefa*) mimic the fluttering and circular flight of the
dove. *Song of Songs Rabba* addresses the anxieties of
the allegorical dove as she hides in the cleft from Pharaoh but rapidly moves on to the delightful salvation
by the Red Sea.[24] HaLevi's dove, by contrast, hovers in
the realm of tormented love, fraught with fear and ambivalence that will not vanish. The dove circles her divine lover and dreams of the "Time of the End," of redemption, but her designs are confounded. Over the
years, she "descends" with despair, vowing "never again
to mention His name," but is unable to extinguish the
fire that stubbornly continues to burn in her heart.
"Why be like her foes?" asks the speaker, breaking in
all of a sudden as the spokesman of the dove. Refusing

to despair, he ends with a desperate plea for God to "come / and not be still," to reveal himself in the midst of his flaming "storms of fire."

The theme of exile found in the Hebrew poetry of al-Andalus evokes more than the diasporic position of the Jews after their expulsion from the Land of Israel. Banishment became a concrete experience for Spanish Jewry after the North African Almoravids conquered al-Andalus in 1090. HaLevi, like many other Jewish refugees, spent a good number of years wandering between different cities in al-Andalus until settling in Castile, which was then under the tolerant rule of King Alfonso VI. In responding to his own historical context, HaLevi does something that is rare in the Midrash. The only history that mattered to the rabbis was sacred history, but in medieval Hebrew poetry, the articulation of the relevance of the ancient text to current events becomes a standard component of the interpretive endeavor.

Another great innovator of medieval liturgical poetry was the poet and philosopher Shelomo Ibn Gabirol (c. 1020–c.1057). Most renowned are his vivid dramatizations of the dialogue between the lovers upon the handles of the lock from Song 5 within a poetic allegorical framework.

Open the Gate

Open the gate, my beloved—
     arise and open the gate:
my spirit is shaken and I'm afraid.
My mother's maid has been mocking me

and her heart is raised against me,
so the Lord would hear her child's cry.
From the middle of midnight's blackness,
    a wild ass pursues me,
as the forest boar has crushed me.
And the end which has long been sealed
    only deepens my wound,
and no one guides me—and I am blind.[25]

At Ibn Gabirol's locked gate, gender roles are inverted. It is the feminine Community of Israel who is asking her divine beloved, her divine *dod*, to open the lock (*sha'ar petach dodi*). Though the scene has somber overtones in the Song itself—the disappearance of the lover and the violence of the guardians of the wall—here these darker shades become "midnight blackness." The beloved's spirit is shaken, and her enemies (the wild ass and the forest boar stand for Islam and Christianity) crush her ruthlessly. Adding insult to injury, the Lord who should have rescued Israel leaves her helpless and blind, with no one to guide her. Love has gone awry, with no clear date for messianic deliverance (similar to the sealed "time of the end" in Daniel 8:17) and no clear indication that the gate of redemption can be opened.[26]

Ibn Gabirol knocks on this heavenly gate once again in "The Gate Long Shut."

The Gate Long Shut

"The gate long shut—
    Get up and throw it wide;

The stag long fled—
>   Send him to my side.

When one day you come
>   To lie between my breasts,
>   That day your scent
>   Will cling to me like wine."

"How shall I know his face, O lovely bride,
>   The lover you are asking me to send?
>   A ruddy face, and lovely eyes?
>   A handsome man to see?"

"Aye, that's my love! Aye, that's my friend!
Anoint that one for me!"[27]

If it weren't for its final two lines, "The Gate Long Shut" could be read as a strikingly erotic secular love poem, imbued with the vocabulary of the Song. It beautifully illustrates the flexible boundaries between the secular and the liturgical in medieval Hebrew poetry but is also representative of a greater insistence on the literal even within an allegorical setting. There are three different figures in this poem: the Community of Israel in the role of the beloved, God as lover, and the stag or gazelle as the Messiah. But the latter two tend to blend into each other. The beloved is endowed with the opening note. She requests, or demands, that her divine lover send back the stag that has fled. And then, in a dreamy tone, she envisions a future encounter with her divine lover (or is it the messianic stag?), whose memorable scent on that glorious day will leave

FIGURE 2. Shlomo Ibn Gabirol's "Shalom to You My Beloved"
(*Shalom Lekha Dodi*). One of Gabirol's most renowned liturgical
poems, whose source of inspiration is the Song of Songs. Courtesy
of the British Library, Cairo Geniza, Or. 10841.

an indelible trace between her breasts (Song 1:13). The
third stanza sounds like a question posed by the divine
lover, who asks the bride (much like the daughters of
Jerusalem in Song 5:9) to depict her loved one. We
would expect him to ask whether the lover she seeks is
"white and ruddy" (Song 5:10), but Ibn Gabirol takes

an unanticipated route. Instead of another echo of the Song we get an evocation of 1 Samuel 16:12, where David is depicted as handsome and "ruddy." It is only here that the allegorical dimension of the poem becomes visible: the yearned-for loved one *is none other than* the Davidic Messiah. The stag procrastinates (a well-known messianic trait), but the gate in this poem is not as tightly sealed as that of "Open the Gate." The more hopeful and playful aspects of Song 5 (the exchange between the Shulamite and the daughters of Jerusalem) are underscored, intimating that the divine lover may ultimately be found.

Alongside poems of longing for the divine lover, medieval Hebrew poets also composed poems depicting the soul's quest for her source. Here too the vocabulary of the Song served as a revered treasure from which to draw images and metaphors. Ibn Gabirol is not the only medieval Hebrew poet to render the soul's seeking of her celestial source in Neoplatonic fashion, but he is the most distinguished. His treatise on metaphysics, *Fountain of Life* (indebted to Greco-Arabic philosophy), is in fact one of the major Neoplatonic works of medieval philosophy.[28] And even though Ibn Gabirol tackles the subject of the soul's yearning to return to her source mostly in his philosophical writings, he occasionally explores her tumultuous trajectory in his poetry as well. In the following poem, the soul craves to return to the divine source of life (and water), from whence she originally emanated, just as the lovesick Shulamite is eager to find her loved one:

> Can anyone praise her all her due?
> Who can deny her beauty and perfection?
> Answer quickly, Lord, a girl sick with love!
> "Gently, my daughter! From the waters of my salvation
> You will surely drink, for you are my Awesome One."[29]

The soul is not only as lovesick as the Shulamite but also as "awesome" (*ayuma*). Like the beloved, the soul too is praised for being as daunting as that which looms on high (*ayuma ka-nidgalot*; Song 6:4), as an emblem of beauty and perfection. The Lord, who in this case actually responds, cannot but assure her that she will ultimately be granted the salvific gift of drinking from the craved-for celestial waters.[30]

The Zohar's Ultimate Song: The Descent of the Shekhinah

There are distinct mystical trends in medieval Hebrew poetry—particularly within the liturgical poetry of Yehuda HaLevi and Ibn Gabirol—but full-scale Jewish mysticism in the Middle Ages emerged only in the late twelfth century, culminating in the composition of the Zohar in thirteenth-century Spain. Written in midrashic style in Aramaic, or Zoharic Aramaic, the Zohar is an exegetical compendium supposedly composed in the circle of Rabbi Shimon, son of Yohai, a famous Tanna of the second century CE. For many centuries the Zohar was accepted as an authentic commentary of late antiquity, but its pseudepigraphic character was laid bare in the twentieth century by the renowned scholar of Kabbalah Gershom Scholem.[31] In one of the foundational studies of Kabbalah, Scholem designated the kabbalist Moshe de León (c. 1240–1305) as the true author of the Zohar. Subsequent generations of Kabbalah scholars modified Scholem's findings, regarding the Zohar as the product of the collective creativity of Moshe de León and his fellow exegetes.[32]

Within the tomes of the Zohar lies another climactic chapter in the story of the Jewish reception of the Song. The kabbalists were familiar with their precursors' poetry and allegorical adaptations of the Song but rarely disclosed the fact. In the Zoharic corpus, where there is a deliberate concealment of the work's actual context, these omissions are understandable. But even in other kabbalistic writings of the period there are only dim references to medieval poets, probably because poetry (and all the more so lyrical poetry) was not considered a relevant genre for exegesis.[33] But influence is not necessarily intentional, linear, or direct. We may assume that the very fact that the Zoharic writers devote significant attention to the literal and the sexual in their commentaries on the Song is indebted in part to the intricate interplay between secular and sacred loves in medieval liturgical poetry.

While the impact of medieval Hebrew poetry remains veiled in the Zoharic Song, the debt to midrashic exegesis is flaunted boisterously throughout. The Zohar's mimicking of the Midrash, however, is accompanied by radical departures. The Zoharic adaptation of Rabbi Akiva's proclamation that "the whole world is not worth the day on which the Song of Songs was given to Israel, for all the Writings are holy, and the Song of Songs is the Holy of Holies" (Mishnah Yadayim 3.5) will serve as our opening note:

> The day that this song was revealed was the same day that *Shekhinah* descended to earth.... On that very day ... and by the Holy Spirit Solomon uttered the praise of this song, which is totality of the whole Torah, totality of the whole work of Creation, totality of mystery of the patriarchs, totality of the exile in Egypt— and when Israel went out of Egypt, and the praise at the Sea—totality of the Ten Commandments and standing at Mount Sinai, and Israel's wandering in the desert until they entered the land and the Temple was built ... totality of Israel's exile among the nations and their redemption.... Whatever was, whatever is, and whatever will eventually be ... is all in Song of Songs.[34]

This is utterly wild. The Zohar takes Rabbi Akiva's definition of the Song of Songs as Holy of Holies and bolsters it with all-encompassing extravagance as it moves from one "totality" to the next. The links that the sages of *Song of Songs Rabba* meticulously mapped out— primarily between the Song and the grand events of the Exodus—proliferate way beyond the midrashic scope. Not only is "the whole work of Creation" added to the list, but so too are messianic times. To top it all, the final pitch positions the Song as omnipresent in every imaginable temporal zone: "Whatever was, whatever is, and whatever will eventually be . . . is all in Song of Songs."

Without one primary event, however, the ultimate Song of Solomon could not have been composed: the appearance of the glamorous Shekhinah. Or, in Zoharic terms: "The day that this song was revealed was the same day that *Shekhinah* descended to earth." The Shekhinah is mentioned in the Midrash as an emblem of divine presence, but only in the Zohar does she rise to the status of a full-fledged feminine force within the godhead.[35] The dramatic introduction of a celestial female figure in the Zohar leads to the formation of a radically different exegetical framework. The midrashic allegory of God as lover and the Community of Israel as the beloved is now projected onto the mystical world of *sefirot*, of divine emanations, and above all onto the primary celestial couple: the Shekhinah and the blessed Holy One. The Shekhinah, the lowest emanation in the supernal tree of the *sefirot*, looms large in Zoharic exegesis, for she is both the consort of the blessed Holy One and the agent of the flow of love between the divine and human worlds.

To better understand why the Song is said to have been first uttered by Solomon on the sublime day of the Shekhinah's descent, let us consider another Zoharic commentary:

Rabbi Yose opened, saying, *Song of Songs, which is Solomon's* (Song of Songs 1:1). This song was aroused by Solomon when the Temple was built and all worlds were consummated, above and below, in single perfection. Although the Companions differ on this, still this song was uttered solely in completeness, when the moon became full and the Temple was constructed according to the pattern above. When the Temple was built below, since the day that the world was created there has never been such joy before the blessed Holy One as on that day.[36]

In *Song of Songs Rabba*, as we've seen, there are two major schools: those who construe the day of the crossing of the Red Sea as the day on which the Song was first sung and those who favor Mount Sinai. The Zoharic Rabbi Yose joins the debate (as if he were living in the Tannaitic period) but then veers from the midrashic context.[37] Against the opinions of the "Companions" (that is, the sages), Rabbi Yose claims that this ultimate song must have been composed and sung at the moment of perfection when King Solomon completed the Temple and Shekhinah descended to dwell on earth. In locating the Song in the Solomonic Temple, the Zohar does not seek historical precision but rather strives for spiritual precision. Only in Solomon's time, when the Temple was fully constructed reflecting the pattern of the heavenly Temple above, was it possible for the Shekhinah to emerge in all her glory and dwell among her people in the most sacred site on earth.[38] The full glory of the celestial Shekhinah on this remarkably joyful day is represented by the full moon, *levana*, one of her most prominent symbols, based on Song 6:10: "Fair as the moon."

The Zoharic Solomon is regarded as the one who can best orchestrate the sexual union between the male and female facets of the godhead; it is only he who can induce the sacred marriage and sexual union between the Shekhinah and the blessed Holy One, allowing bounty to descend from the upper spheres to the world below.[39] But this process is, of course, reciprocal: Solomon is inspired by the Shekhinah, and she in turn yields to his song of love.

The Secret Lover of the Torah: The Exegetical Courtship Scene

The Torah too is drawn into the amorous vortex of the Zohar. Often construed as a beloved of sorts, she is imagined as a beautiful maiden whose love must be sought.[40] In one of the most famous parables of the Zohar, the dialogue between the lovers upon the handles of the lock in Song 5 is refashioned as a scene of exegetical courtship:

> This may be compared to a beloved maiden, beautiful in form and appearance, concealed secretly in her palace. She has a single lover unknown to anyone—except to her, concealedly. Out of the love he feels for her, this lover passes by her gate constantly, lifting his eyes to every side. Knowing that her lover is constantly

circling her gate, what does she do? She opens a little window in that secret palace where she is, reveals her face to her lover, and quickly withdraws. . . . None of those near the lover sees or notices, only the lover, and his inner being and heart and soul follow her. He knows that out of love for him she revealed herself for a moment to arouse him. . . .

Come and see! This is the way of Torah: At first, when she begins to reveal herself to a person, she beckons him momentarily with a hint. If he perceives, good; if not, she sends for him. . . . As he approaches, she begins to speak with him from behind a curtain she has drawn, words suitable for him, until he reflects little by little: This is *derasha*. Then she converses with him from behind a delicate sheet, words of riddle, and this is *haggadah*.

Once he has grown accustomed to her, she reveals herself to him face-to-face, and tells him all her hidden secrets . . . concealed in her heart since primordial days. . . . Then he sees that one should not add to these words or diminish them. Then *peshat* of the verse, just like it is. One should not add or delete even a single letter. So human beings must be alert, pursuing Torah to become her lover, as has been said.[41]

The writers of the Zohar must have admired the same kind of chivalric tales that enthralled Don Quixote. In their account, the Torah, much like the beautiful medieval courtly maiden, doesn't make her lover's life easy. This is partially true of the Shulamite as well, who remains behind the door as she utters words of love to her lover before rushing out into the streets to search for him.

Once the Torah is set in the role of the beloved, courting and learning intermingle. And, in the spirit of the Song, courtship is mutual. The secret lover circles the Torah's gate (his soul yearns to learn), and the Torah in her turn tries to lure him step by step. The lover may not be able to grasp the preliminary hints she provides (the plain sense of the text), but there are other exegetical modes from which he can draw: the *derasha* (midrash) and *haggadah* (philosophical allegory). Only after he has become familiar with these elementary interpretive layers does she reveal her innermost secrets: *sod* (esoteric exegesis).[42]

But then, in an unexpected swerve, the most mystical way of the *sod* leads back to the primary *peshat*, the literal sense, to the simple words on the page, now revealed, more radiant than ever, before the eyes of the true lover of Torah. Broadly speaking, the *derasha*, the *haggadah*, and the *sod* are all allegorical insofar as they search for the hidden truths behind the text and regard the Song as a divine love poem. But what should we make of the proximity of the *sod* to the literal? This is not quite Ibn Ezra's contextual, rational *peshat*, but rather a curious mystical plain sense that dismantles previous definitions of the distinction between the literal and the allegorical.

The Zohar's attempt to distinguish itself from former allegories leads Gershom Scholem to reject the very use of the term "allegory" to define Zoharic exegesis. In *Major Trends in Jewish Mysticism* he defines the symbol—rather than allegory—as the privileged trope of Kabbalah:

> In the mystical symbol a reality which in itself has, for us, no form or shape becomes transparent and, as it were, visible, through the medium of another reality which clothes its content with visible and expressible meaning. . . . The thing which becomes a symbol retains its original form and its original content. It does not become, so to speak, an empty shell into which another content is poured; in itself, through its own existence, it makes another reality transparent which cannot appear in any other form. If allegory can be defined as the representation of an expressible something by another expressible something, the mystical symbol is an expressible representation of something which lies beyond the sphere of expression and communication.[43]

Following in the footsteps of Goethe, Scholem does not do much justice to allegory—after all, in refined allegories of all times there is nothing mechanical or empty. His observations, however, shed light on the ways in which kabbalistic hermeneutics strive to move beyond earlier allegorical modes, bringing together the mystical and the literal in an attempt to fashion a new sense of reality.

The Zoharic writers do not mention medieval Hebrew poetry in the parable of the maid as one of the former exegetical modes on which they rely. But in seeking a new kind of literalism upon the handles of the Torah's lock, they must have been—however partially—inspired by the tremendous tangibility of the erotic fervor found in medieval liturgical adaptations of Song 5.

The Diminishing of the Moon: Times of Exile

The hidden debt of the Zohar's writers to medieval liturgical poets may also be discerned in their occasional use of the Song to underscore the misery of exile. They primarily drew on the somber adaptations of the Song in the Midrash (especially those of *Lamentations Rabba*), but how could anyone remain unmoved by poems such as HaLevi's "A Dove in the Distance" or Ibn Gabirol's "The Gate Long Shut"? Even if the Zoharic writers were not aficionados of lyrical poetry, the exquisite personal renditions of exilic sorrows in medieval Hebrew poetry most likely added a special intensity to the Zohar's representations of the Shekhinah's amorous agonies.[44]

One of the darkest evocations of the Song in the Zohar leads us back to the moon. In exilic times, when the sins of Israel deprive her of the bounty of the upper spheres, the Shekhinah's legendary lunar light diminishes until it becomes a black dot in the sky, almost invisible. At that dark moment, she declares, "Black am I" (*shehora 'ani*), expressing her agony through the Shulamite's memorable words (Song 1:5).[45] Note that the Shekhinah does not cite the entire verset: "Black am I but comely."[46] Beauty seems to have vanished with the light. She stops at *yud*, the final letter of the word "I," *'ani*, given that this miniature letter (indeed, the tiniest letter of the Hebrew alphabet) is entirely black, having no whiteness within. As such, it leaves no space for the Shekhinah to fulfill her protective duty and spread her wings as a celestial mother-bride. The advantage of using the Song antithetically to spell out the sorrows of amorous crises is that one can still preserve a sense of hope for reparation, a hope that the words—and even the letters—of the ancient love poem will ultimately liberate themselves from exilic constriction and return to their original, radiant stature.

The kabbalists do not merely hope for redress. They are mystical "activists," as it were, whose objective is theurgic: to mend the separation between the Shekhinah and the blessed Holy One, as well as between the Shekhinah and the human sphere.[47] This fissure is viewed not quite or only as a historical exile, but rather as a mystical crisis that calls for human intervention. The wildest dream of every kabbalist is to induce the sacred marriage of the celestial couple. The verb *'ur* (to "rouse" or "arouse")—one of the key verbs in the Song—serves as a prominent theurgic code. The Zoharic companions are called upon to mimic the Shulamite, whose heart stirs even when she sleeps, and to seek the heightened intensity of spiritual wakefulness.

Already in *Song of Songs Rabba*, Rabbi Akiva assumes the role of the Shulamite in seeking God's esoteric chambers, but within the context of Zoharic exegesis, such mystical experiences are unabashedly cast as erotic: proximity to the celestial spheres is defined in overtly sexual terms. Once the companions reach a state of arousal they must move on to stimulate the Shekhinah. The goal is to bring the Shekhinah to the point of arousal at which her feminine waters gush forth, a prerequisite for drawing the blessed Holy One into the amorous scene.

How do the kabbalists actually arouse celestial love? Roaring is one of the most peculiar kabbalist techniques that is used in the acute condition in which the Shekhinah's light diminishes. By imitating the roars of lions (taking their cue from Psalms 104:21), the kabbalists deliver a wakeup call to the Shekhinah's divine consort, making him realize that his beloved is in distress. He then approaches her, dark and minuscule as she is, and replenishes her original splendor with his animating, joyful scents and kisses.[48] The Zohar's quest for marital harmony in heaven is a quest for a state of redemption in which there shall be perfection above and below and all worlds shall be united in one bond. But given that the end of exile and messianic times are set in a distant future, the race to increase the Shekhinah's lunar light is forever part of the kabbalist's exegetical expeditions.

Between the Shekhinah and Mary: The Rose

The Zoharic companions seem to roam about in an entirely secluded sacred geography—immersed in theurgic practices while wondering about the inscrutable *sefirot* of the upper spheres—but they are not unaware of some of the new trends in the surrounding Christian world of Castile. The rise of the Shekhinah as the feminine principle of the godhead in thirteenth-century Spain may have been a Jewish response to the growing popularity of the cult of Mary in southern France and northern Spain.[49] It is, however, difficult to assess the degree of cross-cultural exchange with any certainty. The kabbalists of Castile, unlike the poets of Andalusia, would never have admitted their debt to non-Jewish traditions, but they must have been at least partially exposed to the rise of Mary as a deified mother and as the cherished Bride of the Song in the popular culture that surrounded them—whether manifested in street processions, sacred dramas enacted on her holy days, or roadside shrines.[50]

Traces of Christian influence seem to be particularly evident in the centrality of the rose as one of the symbols of the Shekhinah (alongside the moon). Song 2:1–2 is the springboard for the Christian association of Mary with the rose and the lily. She often appears in Christian iconography with roses or lilies in her hands, and medieval cathedrals usually include a rose window dedicated to the Virgin at the end of a transept or above the entrance. The primary source for the Zohar's association of the Shekhinah with the rose is surely the Midrash, where the "rose among thorns" of the Song stands for the chosenness of the Community of Israel, but Mary's rose could have offered an alluring new specimen of a heavenly flower.[51]

Whether or not the Zoharic writers invented a celestial rose in response to Mary's flower, the portrayal of the Song's rose is among the most spectacular Zoharic feats. The very opening of the Zohar is devoted to the Song's rose:

> Rabbi Hizkiya opened: *Like a rose among thorns, so is my beloved among the maidens* [Song 2:2]. . . . Who is a rose? Assembly of Israel. For there is a rose, and then there is a rose! Just as a rose among thorns is colored red and white, so Assembly of Israel includes judgment and compassion. Just as a rose has thirteen petals, so Assembly of Israel has thirteen qualities of compassion surrounding Her on every side.[52]

The rose of the Shekhinah is pictured as a *Rosa gallica versicolor*, one of the most beautiful striped roses whose petals are crimson splashed on white background. The colorful interplay between the red and the white is seen as representing a blend of judgment and compassion, with the thirteen petals standing for the thirteen attributes of compassion emanating from *Keter*, the highest *sefirah*, where total compassion (untainted by judgment) may be found.[53] "Rose is a rose is a rose is a rose," says Gertrude Stein in a well-known debunking of the Romantics' excessive use of figurative speech and departure from "things as they are." The Zohar's approach is clearly different. It underscores the different layers of the rose, including the literal layer, but puts the esoteric embodiment of the Shekhinah as a rose on a pedestal: "For there is a rose, and then there is a rose!" Here, as elsewhere, the Zohar seems to be yoking the Song's love codes and metaphors to a chariot, dashing off to the celestial spheres with a wildly hyperbolic exegetical imagination that is both serious and incredibly playful.

Beyond Spain: Greeting the Sabbath Queen in Safed

The Songs of medieval Hebrew poetry and the Zohar inspired many poets and kabbalists over the following centuries. One of the most marvelous afterlives of these medieval Spanish traditions appeared in Ottoman Palestine, in a city called Safed. Located on one of the northern ridges of the Galilee, Safed became a thriving center for Jewish mysticism shortly after the expulsion from Spain in 1492. Spanish exiles and later the descendants of those exiles settled there, bringing the Iberian cultural heritage with them in their trunks. But while they preserved former exegetical traditions, they also fostered new ones. Among the greatest innovations of the Safed circle was the invention of full-fledged kabbalistic poetry. Poetry and Kabbalah went

hand in hand in sixteenth-century Safed in unprecedented ways, and as they came together a new chapter
in the Song's life emerged.[54] Shelomo Alkabetz
(c 1505–84), Elazar Azikri (1533–1600), and Israel Najara (1555–1628) composed some of the greatest *piyyutim* on the Song. Being both poets and kabbalists, they
did not hesitate to rely on medieval liturgical poetry as
well as the Zohar in their evocations of the Song. Thus,
Najara provides an exquisite depiction of the absent,
wandering lover, *ledod nadad*, and his sleepless beloved (punning on the Hebrew expression for
insomnia—*nedudei sheina*, literally, "sleep wanderings").[55] Similarly, Azikri's *piyyut* "Soul's Beloved"
(*yedid nefesh*) brings the medieval gazelle back with
Zoharic overtones: "Soul's beloved, merciful father, /
draw your servant to your Will; he'll run to you like a
gazelle."[56]

But the most renowned *piyyut* of the Safed circle is
Shelomo Alkabetz's "Hymn to the Sabbath," *Lekhah
Dodi* (literally, "Come, my beloved"), a liturgical poem
that uses the vocabulary of Song 7:12 as its point of departure and refrain. If in the Song the Shulamite urges
her lover to go out to the fields, here the amorous imperative is a spiritual one: the *dod*, the divine lover, is
urged to greet the Shekhinah, the glorious bride, as she
returns from exile with the coming of the Sabbath.
Every Friday at dusk, bliss is brought back to the world
through the renewal of the erotic bond between the
male and female *sefirot*; every Friday, the flow of divine
bounty is restored through this ritualistic welcoming

of the Shekhinah by both God and the congregation of worshippers.[57]

Hymn to the Sabbath

Come, my beloved, to meet the bride,
we'll greet the Sabbath's arrival . . .

Awake, arise, your light has come,
    Rise up now, awake and shine:
    awake, arise, and utter a song . . .

Come in peace—O crown to her husband—
    in joyfulness come, in gladness, and song;
    among the faithful of this treasured people,
        come, my bride . . . my Sabbath Queen.[58]

Lekhah Dodi has been cherished ever since the sixteenth century and is still sung in diverse Jewish congregations around the world as part of the Sabbath evening service. Those who sing this *piyyut* today may not be aware of its intricate fusion of diverse medieval adaptations of the Song's language of love, but they too, like Alkabetz and his companions, position the ancient poem at the very core of communal life and regard it as an indispensable component of their welcoming of the Sabbath Queen.

Monastic Loves

From Saint Bernard to Santa Teresa

Umberto Eco could have written a sequel to *The Name of the Rose* based on the enigmatic life of the Song of Songs in monasteries and convents.[1] The story of the monastic Song is not as gory as Eco's novel, but it too (especially in its later episodes) entails intrigues, investigations by the Inquisition, and the secret copying and circulation of manuscripts. The greatest mystery of all, however, lies in the very fact that this highly erotic Song was read and reread with tremendous passion by monks and nuns who led rigorous ascetic lives. How could they reject sexuality and at the same time dwell on the minutest details of the ancient love poem's celebration of the body? But this is primarily a question that seems relevant to modern readers. Within the monastic world, the renunciation of worldly pleasures and immersion in spiritual pursuits were regarded as the prerequisite for a better understanding of the Song. Regarding the Song as the greatest riddle of Scripture, monastic exegetes, and above all monastic mystics, perceived themselves to be the best equipped to attempt to decipher the baffling and cryptic verses of the ancient love poem. Who but they, wedded as they were to the Bridegroom and devoted body and soul to divine love, could travel along such arduous exegetical paths?

The Sermons of Bernard de Clairvaux: The Kiss of the Mouth

Saint Bernard de Clairvaux (1090–1153), the Cistercian abbot whom Dante chose as the spiritual guide to the celestial spheres in the climactic ending of *The Divine Comedy*, was the most renowned mystical exegete of the Song within the monastic lineage of the medieval period. The term "Cistercian" derives from *Cistercium*, the Latin name for the village of Cîteaux, near Dijon in eastern France. It was in this village that a group of Benedictine monks founded Cîteaux Abbey in 1098 with the goal of adhering more closely to the Rule of Saint Benedict. Bernard played a major role in this monastic reform as the abbot of a Cistercian monastery he founded in the valley of Clairvaux in 1115. There, in that isolated and rugged region of France, he became the spokesman for a revival of rigorous monastic life and sought to position the path of love at the very center of Christian spirituality.[2]

The monastic Song did not begin with Bernard. Monastic culture had produced commentaries on the Song as far back as late antiquity, but it was only in the

Middle Ages—and to a large extent due to the charismatic leadership of Bernard—that this exegetical line became a substantive corpus within Latin literature.[3] In fact, the Song was among the most frequently interpreted biblical texts in medieval Christianity. Curiously enough, this growing interest in the Song in the cloister was not unrelated to the emergence of the new genre of courtly love literature in twelfth-century France. Regardless of the distinct differences between monastic and courtly love, love was in the air in a new way, creating an urgent need to redefine the relationship between body and soul, as well as between earthly and spiritual amorous pursuits.[4]

The Song seems to have been continually on Bernard's mind. Early in his monastic career, when he spent some time in a hut in the monastery's garden convalescing from an illness, he engaged in lengthy conversations on the Song with his close friend William of St. Thierry, seeing the ancient love poem as a vital remedy. In 1135 he began to write a series of sermons in Latin on the Song, *Sermones Super Cantica Canticorum*, which he continued to work on, at intervals, until his death in 1153.[5]

Bernard's eighty-six sermons stay close to Origen's *Commentary*. Like Origen, he too devotes astonishingly elaborate attention to the opening kiss and does not go much beyond Song 2 (with a few leaps into other chapters). More significantly, Bernard adopts Origen's view of the Song as a wedding song celebrating the spiritual union of the Bride and Bridegroom.

But if Origen's commentary revolves around the double nuptial dramas of the Church-Christ (the historical line) and the Soul-Logos (the tropological line), Bernard's sermons give preference to the latter. A landmark in the history of tropological readings of the Song, Bernard's sermons add a distinct monastic flavor to previous explorations of the soul's pursuit of amorous union with the Bridegroom.

From the very outset, in Sermon 1, Bernard makes clear that his commentary on the Song is to be regarded as "spiritual food" that is meant solely for a monastic elite, for those who are capable of relinquishing worldly goods and engaging in spiritual contemplation day and night:

> To you, brothers, different things should be said than to those of the world, and certainly in a different way. Indeed to them milk is given to drink, but not food, as is the method of the Apostle in teaching. For to the spiritual a more solid [food] ought to be given, as that same one teaches by his example: "We speak," he says, "not in the words of those trained in human wisdom, but in the doctrine of the Spirit, bringing together spiritual things with spiritual people" (1 Corinthians 2:13) And again: "We speak wisdom among the perfect," (1 Corinthians 2:6) among whom, I am confident, you are to be found, unless in vain you have long been occupied with heavenly studies, trained your senses, and meditated on the law of God by night and day.[6]

This is not an impersonal address. Bernard speaks in the first person to a chosen audience, his "brothers." They are not laymen; they can have real spiritual food (rather than milk), for they are among the "perfect" to whom one can "speak wisdom," as Paul puts it.[7]

Once Bernard positions the Song as the ultimate guide to Cistercian spiritual perfection, he goes on to probe the primary enigma of the Song.

> Tell us, I beg, by whom, about whom, and to whom is said, "Let him kiss me with the kiss of his mouth"? Why this sudden and abrupt beginning in the middle of a speech? . . . Then again, if she asks for or demands a kiss from someone, why does she clearly and specifically say "with his mouth," as if lovers were in the habit of kissing with anything but their mouth, or with mouths which are not their own? . . .
>
> What a delightful way of putting it . . . ! We begin with a kiss, and the lovely face of Scripture readily attracts the reader and leads him on, so that he delights to search into what lies hidden in it even if it costs him effort, and no difficulty can weary him where the sweetness of the discourse eases the labor. Surely this way of "beginning without a beginning," this freshness of expression in so old a book, must capture the reader's attention? It is clear that this work was not written by human wit, but was composed by the art of the Spirit.[8]

Reading the Song is a labor of love. Every detail is a riddle that requires exegetical effort. But those who

endure the difficulties will discover a ravishing "sweetness of discourse." With refined literary sensitivity
Bernard spells out the delightfully perplexing features
of the Song's opening: the unidentified voices, the curious emphasis on "his mouth" in the depiction of the
kiss, and the abruptness of it all—a "beginning without a beginning" that draws us into the midst of a captivating amorous discourse. Such a superb poem, such
"freshness of expression," he concludes, couldn't but
have been written by "the art of the Spirit."

Let us zoom in with Bernard to explore this opening kiss. He rightly wonders about the unusual reference to the lover's mouth: "As if lovers were in the
habit of kissing with anything but their mouth, or with
mouths which are not their own?" The mention of the
mouth in Song 1 is indeed superfluous, but as such it
highlights the sensuality of the kiss and the power of
love to make every bodily feature of the lover matter.
Bernard neither shies away from the physicality of the
kiss nor hesitates to regard the human amorous contact as a springboard to understanding the verse. For
Bernard, the body is vital to the contemplation of essential truths, enhancing the soul's capacity for ecstasy.
Already in Origen we find a perception of the opening
kiss as a token of divine intimacy, but nowhere in the
Commentary is the body as tangible as it is in Bernard's
sermons.

In Christian exegesis, as in Jewish exegesis, the literal and the bodily become far more pronounced in
the Middle Ages, but for other reasons. It may seem

shocking to modern readers of medieval commentaries on the Song to encounter such fleshly language amid flesh-denying depictions of spiritual union, but one should bear in mind that this flagrant exploration of bodily images was inextricably connected to a growing emphasis on the humanity of Christ.[9] If Christ's body could bleed, die, feed, and give life, if Christ's incarnation in the flesh was perceived as his greatest gift to humanity, what could be more appropriate than to search for spiritual insights via the salvific body?

The question of the kiss continues to occupy Bernard in subsequent sermons as he maps out a series of ascending spiritual kisses—from the kiss of the feet to the kiss of the hand and finally the ultimate kiss of the mouth. The kiss of the feet is a beginner's kiss, the first stage of penitence, marked by a gesture of utter humility. The more advanced devotee may reach the hand. Only then comes the ecstatic kiss of the mouth, the most mystical moment of all, a rare experience given only to the perfect: "And finally, when we shall have obtained these favors through many prayers and tears, we humbly dare to raise our eyes to his mouth, so divinely beautiful, not merely to gaze upon it, but—I say it with fear and trembling—to receive its kiss."[10] If the beloved asks to be kissed with the kisses of the mouth, it is for a reason: she is well aware of the existence of other modes of kissing and is eager to experience the grandest kiss of all. It is only at this elevated stage— after moving from a "mere gaze" to the touch of lips—that the monastic devotee can hope to approach

FIGURE 3. Christ and the Church kiss. A visual allegorical interpretation of the opening kiss of the Song of Songs, twelfth century. From Bede, *In Cantica Canticorum*, Cambridge, King's College MS. 19 f. 12v. Reproduced by permission of the Provost and Scholars of King's College, Cambridge.

the Neoplatonic ideal of prompting the soul's return to her source.

"Saw Ye Him Whom My Soul Loveth?": Spiritual Affect

Affect, no less than the body, is a pivotal element in Bernard's personalistic spirituality of love. He constantly uses the words *affectio*, *afficere*, *affectus*, highlighting the indispensability of affect to spiritual experience. Such affect is utterly feminized, not only because of the embodiment of the soul as Bride, but also because the term for soul in Latin, *anima*, is grammatically feminine. Writing for his fellow monks, Bernard urges them to adopt the role of the Bride, the *sponsa*, and to envision their spiritual quest in feminine terms. This instruction may sound peculiarly homoerotic, but from Bernard's perspective, it is precisely the kind of gender fluidity that is necessary for fostering the soul and its affective dimension.[11]

Bernard's exploration of affective spiritual zeal reaches a unique peak of eloquence in the emotionally charged sermons devoted to verses in the Song such as Song 3:3, where the term *anima* actually appears: *num quem dilexit anima mea vidistis* ("Saw ye him whom my soul loveth?"). Bernard relies on the Vulgate, the Latin translation of the Bible that prevailed in the medieval monastic world, but the canonical English translation of the King James Version quoted here also adheres to the spiritual path with its use of "soul." Translation is forever intertwined with interpretation. *Anima* or "soul" are the preferable translations of the Hebrew *nefesh* within a traditional allegorical mindset, but they are not the only options. The term *nefesh* in biblical Hebrew has multiple meanings: "breath of life," "life," and "innermost feelings," as well as "soul." In recent translations, the Shulamite's question in 3:3 is rendered as "Have you seen him? Have you seen the one I love?" (Blochs) or "Have you seen him I love so?" (Alter). A literalist translation of the expression *et she-ahava nafshi* into English is by no means an easy task. The Shulamite could have said, "Have you seen my loved one?" but she adds her *nefesh* to the scene as the agent of love to underscore the intense sense of innermost feelings, of a love that rocks her entire being from within. Each one of these modern translations attempts to render this emotional intensity differently: the Blochs translation relies on the repetition of the question, while Alter's rendition achieves this effect through its addition of "so." But such literalism is a modern phenomenon that became prominent only in the twentieth century. For anyone in the Middle Ages whose spiritual food was provided by the Vulgate, Song 3:3 couldn't but serve as clear-cut proof that the ancient love poem revolves around the amorous pursuits of the *anima*.

Consider the opening lines of Bernard's commentary on Song 3:3 in Sermon 79:

> "Have you seen him whom my soul loves?" O strong and burning love, O love urgent and impetuous, which does not allow me to think of anything but you. . . . You throw order into confusion, ignore moderation; you laugh at all considerations of fitness, reason, modesty and prudence. . . . All the Bride's thoughts and words are full of nothing but your music and fragrance, so completely have you taken possession of her heart and tongue. "Have you seen him whom my soul loves?" she asks—as though they would know what she meant. Who is it whom your soul loves, for whom you enquire? Has he no name? . . . I speak like this because of the strange manner of

speech and extraordinary disregard for names, quite different from the rest of Scriptures. But in this marriage-song it is not the words which are to be pondered, but the affections behind them. . . . And love speaks everywhere; if anyone desires to grasp these writings, let him love. It is vain for anyone who does not love to listen to this song of love, or to read it, for a cold heart cannot catch fire from its eloquence.[12]

The Shulamite is the one to embody most forcefully the emotional intensity of the *nefesh* in the Song (in fact, she is the only one who repeatedly uses the term *nefesh*), and Bernard is well aware of this. He merges with the Shulamite as she wanders at night in the streets in search of her loved one and spells out her tumultuous affections with exclamatory ruminations: "O strong and burning love, O love strong and impetuous, which does not allow me to think of anything but you." If it weren't for the spiritual framework of his sermons, we could easily regard his depiction of an all-consuming, overbearing love, one that takes possession of the "heart and tongue," as a poignant depiction of earthly love. But this is Bernard's claim to fame: the capacity to ignite spiritual love with a full-blown depiction of human affect.

Here too Bernard is attentive to the complications of the text. The Bride, the soul, asks the watchmen whether they have seen her loved one without mentioning his name. In the Song itself, this namelessness adds to the dreamy quality of the text—in dreams no explanations are needed—but also to the experience of being wrapped up in love to the extent of assuming that everyone else is equally preoccupied with the lover's whereabouts. In Bernard's sermon, the Song's "strange manner of speech" is seen primarily as an invitation to search beyond words and names, beyond rational pondering, in the realm of the affections that blaze behind the scriptural text. Without the experience of love, without the capacity to go beyond language toward the ineffable, Bernard insists, the Song remains out of reach, and so does divine love.

Affect is akin to desire. But whereas desire underscores lack, affect acknowledges lack while giving greater importance to the movement toward the other in search of reciprocity.[13] In Bernard's world of affect, love is primarily a divine initiative, a call for human response, a call to move toward the Other. The Song was written with divine love, and so love is the only path through which to ascend toward the divine Word (no "cold heart" can catch the fire). Such mutuality is further highlighted at a later point in this sermon devoted to the subsequent verse, Song 3:4—"It was but a little that I passed from them [the watchmen], but I found him whom my soul loveth: I held him, and would not let him go, until I had brought him into my mother's house." The Bride, writes Bernard, says "'I held him,' . . . [y]et in her turn she is held by the one whom she holds."[14] Her affection is by definition a response to being already loved and held by the divine spouse. No one can seek God who has not already been found by God.

Immersed in this contemplative search for divine love, Bernard may seem like one who has never left the cloister. But in fact the Cistercian abbot was involved in fierce theological disputes and was influential in the broader political sphere as well, serving as the spiritual engine behind the Second Crusade. Canonized in 1174, Bernard produced a series of writings on spiritual love that remain among his lasting legacies. His sermons had a tremendous impact on the growth of the Latin genre of commentaries on the Song in the Middle Ages, as well as on the development of a greater body of mariological liturgies hailing Mary as *sponsa*. But his quest for mystical union also had a ripple effect way beyond the Middle Ages, impacting subsequent generations of monastic Christians.

Spanish Mysticism in the Era of Counter-Reformation

Among Bernard's most intriguing followers in the path of spiritual love were three of the towering figures of sixteenth-century Spanish mysticism: Santa Teresa of Ávila (1515–1582), Saint John of the Cross or San Juan de la Cruz (1542–1591), and Fray Luis de León (1527–1591). All three offered new versions of the monastic Song—Teresa and John of the Cross as Discalced Carmelites (a reformed branch of the

Carmelite order) and Luis de León as an Augustinian friar. And although the three were influenced by the writings of other great Christian thinkers and mystics—among them Origen, Augustine, Gregory the Great, and Aquinas—Bernard's *Sermones* left a unique stamp on their work.

In moving from medieval France to sixteenth-century Spain, we shift from Latin to Spanish and from one of the peaks of the monastic Song to the swan song of the tropological mode. In the wake of the Reformation, allegory (and particularly tropological exegesis) lost something of its halo, while the literal sense of Scripture, *sola scriptura*, or "Scripture alone," acquired greater weight. The endorsement of Scripture as the site of authority was accompanied by an endorsement of vernacular translations. For centuries the western church had used the Vulgate, Saint Jerome's Latin translation of the Bible from the fourth century CE, regarding it as synonymous with the biblical text itself. A dramatic change took place in the sixteenth century with the rise of vernacular Bibles—from Martin Luther's 1522 German Bible to the 1539 Coverdale English Bible (based on William Tyndale's earlier translation).[15] Spain lagged behind. Beginning around 1499, its Catholic kings issued several decrees prohibiting the possession and use of vernacular translations, restrictions that continued to be tightened until the Spanish church, having failed to convince the Council of Trent to adopt its motions to ban Scripture in the vernacular, did so unilaterally with its 1551 Index. The reasoning behind this prohibition, as Archbishop Carranza put it, was to prevent unlearned people from falling into error by reading Scripture without guidance.[16] It was against this backdrop of Spain's fervent adherence to Catholic tradition and battle against what the Inquisition perceived as "Lutheran heresy" that Teresa of Ávila, San Juan de la Cruz, and Fray Luis de León put forth some of the most daring and exquisite commentaries on the ancient love poem.

Our focus is on the Christian lineage that runs from Bernard to these three Spanish exegetes, but we should note that all three were of *converso* lineage, born into families of Jews who had been forced to convert to Christianity.[17] In fact, Teresa's paternal grandfather, Juan Sánchez de Toledo, was condemned by the Spanish Inquisition for allegedly returning to the Jewish faith. Some studies suggest that there are kabbalistic undercurrents in the writings of these three mystics, made possible by lingering Jewish traditions within *converso* culture.[18] These studies are somewhat speculative, for there is no clear-cut evidence of kabbalistic themes in their work. But we may assume that, in more diffuse ways, the very passion of the three for the Song and their adherence to a mystical mode of reading could have been inspired not only by Christian traditions but also by the pivotal position of the ancient love poem in kabbalistic exegesis. One can hardly imagine that it is merely a coincidence that the three great monastic mystics of sixteenth-century Spain who wrote commentaries on the Song were all of *converso* lineage.

Santa Teresa's *Meditations*: Nuns as Brides

Though the feminine principle acquired a greater role in medieval Christianity with the deification of Mary and the rise of Mariology, we hear of no female exegete writing on the Song until the sixteenth century.[19] The first woman who ventured to record her meditations on the Song was the renowned reformer of the Carmelite order in Spain: Santa Teresa of Ávila. Written between 1566 and 1571, Teresa's *Meditations on the Song of Songs* (*Meditaciones sobre los Cantares*) provoked a hostile response from the Spanish Inquisition. Domingo Báñez (her primary confessor) signed one of the manuscripts of the *Meditations* to indicate his approval of it, but later Diego de Yanguas (another of Teresa's confessors and a theologian of the Inquisition) instructed her to destroy the manuscript and all copies of it. Relying on Paul's instruction that women should keep silence in the church of God, the inquisitors were determined to eradicate what they perceived as a perilous violation of gender codes. No woman, they declared, was to be permitted to write a commentary on scriptural texts. Teresa was ordered to burn her book, and she did so at once. But her devoted nuns made sure to preserve a copy despite the Inquisition's decree.

Teresa would never have defined herself as the first woman exegete of the Song. Careful to avoid the appearance of violating the Inquisition's restrictions on women reading and interpreting the Bible, she insistently undermines her authority in the opening remarks of her *Meditations*. Addressing the nuns of her convent, she writes:

> I have carefully noted that it seems from what is manifested here that the soul is speaking with one person and asking peace from another. It says: *Let Him kiss me with the kiss of His mouth*; and next, seemingly, it speaks to someone whom it is with. . . . I don't understand why this is; and that I don't understand gives me great delight. Indeed, daughters, the soul will not have to reflect upon the things it seems we can grasp with our lowly intellects here below as intensely as it will upon those that can in no way be understood. . . . Thus I highly recommend that when you read some book or hear a sermon or think about the mysteries of our sacred faith you avoid tiring yourselves or wasting your thoughts in subtle reasoning about what you cannot properly understand. Many things are not meant for women to understand, nor even for men.[20]

Like Bernard, Teresa highlights the enigmatic qualities of the opening verse. But she provides no explanation. Instead of expounding on its meaning, she savors the inscrutability of the divine words and instructs her nuns to know their limits as women, to acknowledge their "lowly intellects" and "avoid tiring" themselves with thoughts on mysteries that remain beyond their ken. To further highlight her lack of erudition, Teresa underscores the fact that she knows no Latin and relies solely on translated passages of the Song into Spanish from the Office of the Virgin, which Carmelite nuns recited daily (the insertion of translations of selected biblical verses into liturgical texts was approved by the Inquisition). Accordingly, Teresa's citations are not always exact and may have been deliberately imprecise. And yet Teresa's declarations of incompetence are, above all, a rhetorical strategy that allows her to survive in an exegetical world that accepts no women.[21] Supposedly innocent of any exegetical aspirations, the *Meditations* nonetheless provides a new mode of reading Scripture and is replete with interpretive insights.

None other than the Virgin Mary is Teresa's role model. In reflecting on the scene of annunciation, Teresa describes the wise Virgin as capable of "surrendering" her "intellects" and accepting the divine Word. Mary first asks the angel, "How can this be?" Yet once he answers, "The Holy Spirit will come upon you, the power of the Most High will overshadow you" (Luke 1:34–35), the Blessed Virgin relinquishes her doubts:

> As one who had such great faith and wisdom, she understood at once that if these two intervened, there was nothing more to know or doubt. She did not act as do some learned men (whom the Lord does not lead by this mode of prayer and who haven't begun a life of prayer), for they want to be so rational about things and so precise in their understanding that it doesn't seem anyone else but they with their learning can understand the grandeurs of God. If only they would learn something from the humility of the most Blessed Virgin![22]

Alongside moments of self-deprecation, Teresa provocatively asserts that this new feminine mode of grasping scriptural truths—so vital to her nuns—can also serve as an alternative to the rational inquiries that trap "learned men." No wonder the Inquisitors were determined to ban the book.[23] These harsh restrictions notwithstanding, we should keep in mind that being a nun was one of the only paths available for women who wanted to write in sixteenth-century Spain (women writers of the Spanish Renaissance were either nuns or aristocrats).

Teresa's meditations are written from a distinctly personal position and directed to her *hijas*, her "daughters," at the convent, whom she invites to come join her in marveling at the exquisite joy and consolation of pursuing divine intimacy through the Song. Her *hijas* are cast in the role of the daughters of Jerusalem, whom Teresa, as the Shulamite, approaches in an attempt to share the intense pleasures and pain of being lovesick.[24] No one before Teresa had conveyed the sense of solidarity and the thrill that underlies the Shulamite's conversation about love with a community of women. The nuns' task, however, is not merely to hear about the loved one but also to take part in the amorous pursuit. Having vowed to be brides of Christ, they are especially suited to follow in the footsteps of the Bride. The monastic dimension of Teresa's address becomes more palpable as she justifies the quest for the divine kiss:

In what better way could we be occupied than to prepare rooms within our souls for our Spouse and reach the stage in which we can ask Him to give us the kiss of His mouth? . . . Oh, my daughters! What a great state of life we are in, for no one but ourselves can keep from saying these words to our Spouse since we took Him for our Spouse when we made our professions.[25]

In the wake of Bernard, Teresa dwells time and again on the details of the opening kiss. And yet there is a distinct difference. Given that Teresa is a woman, her desire to dissolve in the Bridegroom via a kiss sounds far more literal. Realizing the danger of being accused of literalism and Lutheran heresy, she is quick to declare:

People will say I am a fool, that the words [of Song 1:2] don't mean this, that they have many meanings, that obviously we must not speak such words to God, that for this reason it is good that simple people do not read these things. I confess that the passage has many meanings. But the soul that is enkindled with a love that makes it mad desires nothing else than to say these words. Indeed, the Lord does not forbid her to say them. . . . [T]hese words in themselves, taking them only literally, would truly cause fear if the one uttering them were in his senses. But the one whom Your love, Lord, has drawn out of himself, You will truly pardon . . . even though to say them is daring.

> And my Lord, if the kiss signifies peace and friend-
> ship why shouldn't souls ask You for this kiss?[26]

Challenging the conviction of the Counter-Reformation that "simple people"—among them women—are unfit to interpret scriptural texts, Teresa attempts to prove that her reading of Song 1:2 is the true one. It may seem daringly literal, even heretical, but she defends herself as opting for a different kind of literalism that does not remain on the level of the senses, one that seeks divine grace.[27] As such, nothing could be more fitting than to encourage her *hijas* to ask for the Bridegroom's kiss of friendship and union in fulfillment of their vocation.

The Bridegroom's Winelike Milk: Heavenly Inebriation

In quest of mystical union with the Bridegroom, Teresa craves not only his kiss but also his breasts. Why breasts? That "breasts" rather than "love" are hailed as "better than wine" in Teresa's somewhat modified rendition of Song 1:2–3—"Your breasts are better than wine, and give forth the most sweet fragrance" (*Meditations* 4)—is indebted to a mistranslation in the Septuagint, later adopted by the Vulgate (the Hebrew term *dodekha*, "love," was translated as "breasts," *dadekha*, due to a different understanding of the vowels at stake).[28] What seems another odd cross-gendered moment in the exegetical history of the Song—the maternal dimension of the Bridegroom—has been regarded by many generations of exegetes as a natural expression of the multifaceted character of divine benevolence.[29] Both Origen and Bernard devote commentaries to the divine breasts, but neither of them develops the topic to the ecstatic heights evident in Teresa's depiction of the intoxicating experience of tasting the winelike milk of the Spouse:

> Just as a person is caused to swoon from great pleasure and happiness, it seems to the soul it is left suspended in those divine arms, leaning on that sacred side and those divine breasts. It doesn't know how to do anything more than rejoice, sustained by the divine milk with which its Spouse is nourishing it and making it better so that He might favor it, and it might merit more each day. When it awakens from that sleep and that heavenly inebriation, it remains as though stupefied and dazed and with a holy madness. . . . While it was in that intoxication, the soul thought it had no farther to ascend. But when it saw itself in a higher degree and completely drenched in the countless grandeurs of God, and sustained in this way, it makes a delicate comparison and says: *Your breasts are better than wine.*[30]

Teresa breathes life into the Song's wine metaphor. Wine in the Song is never only literal. Once it is defined as comparable to love, every mention of wine—or "wine house" (*beit ha-yayin*), or even vines—sounds like a playful double entendre that underscores the intoxicating power of love.[31] In Teresa's adaptation, the inebriation is that of the soul, but here too there is a notable blurring of the boundaries between literal and figurative drunkenness.

Unlike its earthly counterpart, heavenly inebriation is not easily achieved: it is a process. Initially, the intoxicated soul assumes that it can ascend no more, but gradually it discovers new pinnacles on being drenched progressively with a greater dose (or even overdose) of divine milk-wine. It is then that the soul becomes capable of a metaphoric leap, what Teresa calls "delicate comparison," and utters the words: "*Your breasts are better than wine.*"[32]

And yet the intense pleasure of heavenly inebriation is in Teresa's view inseparable from exposure to the wounding aspects of lovesickness. Love, Teresa goes on to explain, is like an arrow that "must wound His Majesty."[33] But then, after one becomes fixed in God, the wounding amorous arrow is delivered back to the beloved, hurling her into the stupefying death-like suspension of holy inebriation. Swooning in the divine arms is a mode of "dying of love," the soul being slain, as it were, by the excess of the Bridegroom's sweetness.[34] A soul yearning to unite with her Bridegroom for Teresa is forever a soul that experiences the different modalities of love represented in the Song: "swoons, deaths, afflictions, delights, and joys."[35]

Gian Lorenzo Bernini was well aware of the proximity of Teresa's representation of mystical union to a scene of lovemaking. In his well-known sculpture *The Ecstasy of Saint Teresa* (1652), he captures the unique mixture of exhilarating joy and piercing pain, of the bodily and the spiritual, in Teresa's orgasmic encounter with an angel and his spear of love. Bernini's primary source was a passage in Teresa's book *The Life of Saint Teresa of Avila* (written a few years before *Meditations* and providing an account of her life up to 1562):

> In his hands I saw a great golden spear, and at the iron tip there appeared to be a point of fire. This he plunged into my heart several times so that it penetrated to my entrails. When he pulled it out, I felt that he took them with it, and left me utterly consumed by the great love of God. The pain was so severe that it made me utter several moans. The sweetness caused by this intense pain is so extreme that one cannot possibly wish it to cease, nor is one's soul then content with anything but God. This is not a physical, but a spiritual pain, though the body has some share in it—even a considerable share.[36]

This was a climactic vision in Teresa's life—a revelatory moment that would color her subsequent writings and definitely guide her reading of the Song. No other biblical text could provide her with such fertile soil on which to explore the intoxication of divine love, its maddening wounds, and the contact zones between spiritual experiences that are not bodily and those in which the "body has its share."

In 1622, only forty years after her death, Teresa was canonized by Pope Gregory XV. One may well

FIGURE 4. Gian Lorenzo Bernini (Italy, 1598–1680), *The Ecstasy of Saint Teresa* (1651), set in an elevated *aedicule* in the Cornaro Chapel, Santa Maria della Vittoria, Rome.

wonder what made Teresa's canonization possible. Processes of canonization, as we have seen, often include unexpected turns. One possible explanation for Teresa's rise as a saint is the fact that her daring, sensual definition of mystical union was set within a framework of asceticism. Her reform, after all, sought to reinforce stricter, more frugal modes of devotion. Indeed, her order is called the Discalced Carmelites because they preferred being barefoot to partaking of the worldly luxury of the shoe.

The "Spiritual Canticle" of Saint John of the Cross: Pastoral Passions

Saint John of the Cross was not only Santa Teresa's partner in reforming the Carmelite order and invigorating the spirit of the Discalced Carmelites but also a fellow traveler in the exegetical world of the Song. The story of John's "Spiritual Canticle" (*Cántico espiritual*) begins with intrigue and strife within the Carmelite world. On the night of December 2, 1577, a group of Carmelites opposed to reform broke into John's abode in Ávila and took him prisoner. He was jailed in a monastery in Toledo, where he was kept under a harsh regimen that included public lashing on a weekly basis and severe isolation in a narrow, stifling cell measuring six feet by ten, barely large enough for his body.[37] During his nine-month imprisonment, he managed against all odds (using a pen and ink secretly passed to him by the friar who guarded his cell) to compose the bulk of his renowned mystical adaptation of the Song: the "Spiritual Canticle." Shortly after John's escape from prison, his canticle was copied and circulated by Teresa's nuns. Additional stanzas were added over the next few years.[38]

The "Spiritual Canticle" is an eclogue, a pastoral poem, that revolves around a passionate dialogue between the soul as Bride (*alma*) and Christ as Bridegroom (*Amado*). John follows Bernard's individualistic, tropological line but combines it with elements of pastoral poetry, a thriving genre of the Spanish

Renaissance. The *Églogas* (*Eclogues*) of Garcilaso de la Vega and the mystical adaptations of the genre by Sebastiàn de Córdoba were among the sources of inspiration for John's casting of the biblical lovers within bucolic scenes.[39] The Song surely lends itself to such readings, for the two lovers are shepherds, and some of their encounters take place in pastoral meadows. But such bucolic elements do not quite form a genre: they are part of the ever-changing geographies of love in the ancient poem.

Being both a mystic and a poet—in fact, one of Spain's greatest lyric poets—John addresses the question of the suitability of poetry to mystical contemplation in the prologue to his commentary on the "Spiritual Canticle":

> Who can describe in writing the understanding he gives to loving souls in whom he dwells? And who can express with words the experience he imparts to them? Who, finally, can explain the desires he gives them? Certainly, no one can! Not even they who receive these communications. As a result these persons let something of their experience overflow in figures, comparisons and similitudes, and from the abundance of their spirit pour out secrets and mysteries rather than rational explanations.[40]

Since language cannot convey the ineffable experience of a soul in love directly, John claims, the "figures, comparisons and similitudes" of poetry, gushing forth from spiritual experience, are far more effective than rational explanations. The "saintly doctors" (he may be referring to the Carmelite doctors Baconthorpe and Bologna) "can never furnish an exhaustive explanation of these figures and comparisons," but poetry may come closer to the original mode of the Song and thus offer a more intuitive and transcendent encounter with scriptural truths.

The first simile John chooses to evoke in the "Spiritual Canticle" is that of the lover as stag:

> Bride
> Where is it that you hid [*Adonde te escondiste, Amado* ...],
> Beloved, and left me to lament?
> Like the stag you fled,
> having wounded me,
> calling, I came out after you, and you were gone.
>
> Shepherds, who might go
> there through the sheepfold to the hill,
> if you should chance to see
> him whom most I love,
> tell him that I suffer, grieve, and die ...[41]

If medieval Hebrew poets fuse the Song's stag with the gazelle of Arabic poetry, John adds a pastoral color to the trope of the lover. The stag is a common component of eclogues (the *ciervo*, or stag, roams about from the very outset in Garcilaso's first eclogue), appearing usually as a target of the hunt within bucolic landscapes. In John's intriguingly inverted scene of chase, we enter allegorical zones, for the hunted animal becomes a hunter who wounds the Bride/soul and then

flees. The wounds, however, are wounds of love, reminiscent of Christ's wounds borne on behalf of humanity, and as such do not deter her from seeking him.
Quite the contrary—the Bridegroom's arrows of love
spur the Bride to desperately search for the beloved stag
that has called her and then disappeared. The intensity
of affect in the soul's quest for the one whom she loves
calls to mind Bernard's sermons, but, in his dire depictions of the Bride's sufferings and the mutuality of
wounding, John comes closer to Teresa's *Meditations*.

Beyond the metaphor of the lover as stag, many
other echoes of the Song are interwoven in the opening
stanzas of the "Spiritual Canticle" (John relies extensively on the Vulgate but renders his scattered biblical
citations in Spanish).[42] One such echo recalls the first
exchange between the biblical lovers, with its distinct
pastoral flavor: "Tell me, O thou whom my soul loveth,
where thou feedest, where thou makest thy flock to rest
at noon. . . . If thou know not, O thou fairest among
women, go thy way forth by the footsteps of the flock,
and feed thy kids beside the shepherds' tents" (Song
1:7–8). In the Song, the Shulamite asks her adored
shepherd directly where she might find him. In the
"Spiritual Canticle," the loved one is absent, so the beloved addresses her question to the shepherds. Touches
of the darker scenes of Song 3 and Song 5, where the
lover is missing, are introduced by John into Song 1.

The agonies of love and craving to see the Bridegroom become more poignant in later stanzas of the

"Spiritual Canticle," when the Bride, like the lover who seduces his dovelike beloved to come out of the crevices, coaxes her Bridegroom to reveal himself.

> Reveal your presence,
> and let your sight and beauty kill me;
> consider the sickness
> of love, which is not cured
> save by presence and countenance.
>
> Oh crystalline fountain!
> If in these silvered features
> you should suddenly form
> the eyes I long for
> which in my inmost self I have portrayed![43]

In the absence of a response from her hidden lover, the Bride turns to the "crystalline fountain" and imagines an exquisite scene of internal and external reflections. Instead of gazing at her own eyes reflected in the glassy waters, she yearns to encounter the longed-for eyes of the *Amado*, the eyes envisioned in her "inmost self."

After an arduous process of purification, the yearning soul ultimately finds her Bridegroom by the riverside. It is there by the river, whose waters seem to blend with the Bridegroom's wine, that their nuptial bond is celebrated with utter joy.

> In the inner cellar
> of my Beloved I drank, and when I came forth
> along all this riverside

I knew not a thing,
and I lost the flock which formerly I followed.

There he gave me his breast,
there he taught me very appetizing knowledge
and I gave to him indeed
myself, leaving not a thing;
there I promised to be his bride.[44]

This is John's bucolic version of heavenly inebriation. The swoon of beatific forgetfulness leads to a loss of the flock the Bride has formerly herded. But this is not a moment of pastoral irresponsibility; rather, it is a token of spiritual maturity that allows the loving soul to approach mystical union, dissolving in the intoxicating world of the Bridegroom's breast.

John's well-known poem *La noche oscura del alma*, "Dark Night of the Soul," written either during or right after his imprisonment, is another "Spiritual Canticle" of sorts. In this case, however, the Shulamite's nocturnal wanderings are more apparent, serving as the primary point of departure for the soul's search in the dark night.

One dark night,
Fired with love's urgent longings
—Ah, the sheer grace!—
I went out unseen . . .
With no other light as my guide
Than the one that burned in my heart;

This guided me

More surely than the light of noon . . .

Here too the poem revolves around the amorous wanderings of the soul and ends with a sweet scene of
wounding oblivion as the Bride unites with her Bridegroom, "forgotten" among the Song's lilies:

When the breeze blew from the turret
Parting his hair,
He wounded my neck
With his gentle hand,
Suspending all my senses.

I abandoned and forgot myself
Laying my face on my beloved;
All things ceased; I went out of myself,
Leaving my cares
Forgotten among the lilies.[45]

Reflecting on the "Spiritual Canticle," Colin
Thompson comments, "Its images of beauty, freedom
and space—fields, flowers, rivers, mountains and wild
beasts, blowing winds—bear eloquent testimony to
the power of a man's mind to create a world vibrant
with life, light, and colour, even in the deadness of a
prison cell."[46] John's power, we may add, is indebted to
the Song's power. In John's renditions of the Song, we
witness the remarkable capacity of the ancient love
poem to guide its readers to a world teeming with life
even in the darkest nights.

Fray Luis de León's Vernacular Translation of the Song: The Monastic Hebraist

Fray Luis de León—a mystic, poet, theologian, and Bible professor at the University of Salamanca—was an Augustinian friar rather than a Discalced Carmelite, but his life and work intersect with those of Teresa and John in a variety of ways. "I never knew nor saw Mother Teresa de Jesús while she was on earth," Fray Luis wrote to the Discalced Carmelite nuns of Madrid, "but now that she lives in Heaven I know and see her constantly in two vivid images which she has left of herself, and these are her spiritual daughters and her books."[47] Making sure that others would be able to benefit from Teresa's books, he immersed himself in laborious editorial work, collating her manuscripts and preparing the definitive edition of 1588. Fray Luis's contact with John was more nebulous. John may have been Fray Luis's student at Salamanca, where the former studied theology between 1564 and 1567. But whether or not the two were acquainted, they shared much in common—from the perception of the Song as a spiritual eclogue to their determination to write on the Song in prison.

Three years before John's imprisonment by the unreformed Carmelites, Fray Luis was imprisoned by the Inquisition. His troubles began when he translated the Song from Hebrew into Spanish in response to a request by his cousin, Isabel Osorio, a nun at the Salamancan convent of Sancti Spiritus. Like Santa Teresa and other nuns, Isabel had no knowledge of Latin (not to mention Greek or Hebrew) and thus had no direct access to the entire text of the Song. Fray Luis meant his vernacular Song and the accompanying exposition to be a gift for his cousin alone, but it ended up circulating illicitly and eventually fell into the hands of the Inquisition. The Augustinian friar was imprisoned in Valladolid from March 1572 to December 1576, his vernacular translation of the Song being one of his gravest offenses.

When Fray Luis translated the Song into Spanish for Isabel Osorio, he did so despite the Inquisition's ban. In a sense, he was driven by the same belief that motivated Luther. Just as Luther advocated his German Bible as a way of ensuring that the Word of God would become accessible to all, "the mother in the house, the children in the street, the common man in the market," so too Fray Luis could see no justification for restricting the access of nuns to Holy Writ.[48] Later, his willingness to support a different cultural role for women would become evident in his book The *Perfect Marriage* (*La perfecta casada*).[49]

What made Fray Luis's vernacular translation even more controversial is the fact that as a Hebraist he insisted on adhering to the Hebrew original to the extent of deviating occasionally from the Vulgate. Abraham Ibn Ezra's medieval commentary on the Song was among his sources.[50] Fray Luis's *converso* lineage and familiarity with the work of Jewish exegetes made the Inquisitors all the more suspicious that he intended to "Judaize" the biblical text and distort its Christian teachings.[51] His statement that "there are certain places in Sacred Scripture which, if they are read according to the Hebrew or Greek verity, give stronger confirmation to the tenets of our faith, than if they are read as the Vulgate has them" did not quite appease them.[52]

In Fray Luis's *Respuesta* (*Reply*) to the Inquisition, written in prison, he provides elaborate justifications for his approach. The most renowned is his explanation regarding the proper translation of the phrase *mibaad letsamatekh* of Song 4:1, which describes the dovelike eyes of the beloved shining through her hair or veil. Fray Luis translates *tsamatekh* as referring to hair locks: *entre tus cabellos*.[53] His choice contrasts not with "veil" but rather with the Vulgate's obscure rendition: *absque eo quod intrinsecus latet* ("apart from that which lies concealed"). Saint Jerome, Fray Luis explains, misread the term *tsamatekh* as referring to the "shameful" parts of a woman's body (female genitalia) and thus invented a peculiar circumlocution in his Latin translation. Calling for a closer adherence to the Hebrew original and for a linguistic awareness of the complex, multiple meanings of Hebrew words, Fray Luis suggests that when Solomon praises his wife's radiant eyes he refers to the surrounding beauty of her hair with no intention of making a "perilous leap" to the lower part of her body.[54] Another one of Fray Luis's notable corrections (though it is not mentioned in his *Respuesta*) is his translation of Song 1:2. The lover no longer has breasts that are better than wine, for *dodekha* is now translated as *amores*, "love."

If translating the Bible into the vernacular and correcting the Vulgate weren't enough, Fray Luis also ventured to dwell on the literal dimension of the Song, calling attention to the nuances of the *corteza*, the bark or outer layer: "For one has to understand that this Book was originally written in verse, and is all one pastoral eclogue in which Solomon and his Spouse, and at some points their companions, speak in the words and the language of shepherds as though they were all village-dwellers."[55] Such literalism, however, was far from appealing in the Inquisitors' eyes. Fray Vincente Hernández denounced Fray Luis's work to the Inquisition as "a love-letter with no spiritual meaning, scarcely differing at all from the love poetry of Ovid."[56]

In response, Fray Luis provocatively defends his hermeneutic project by reminding his critics that none other than "the Holy Spirit considered it appropriate to use the figure of human love for the love of Christ and the Church."[57] His emphasis on literalism is by no means an attempt to undermine the spirituality of the Song. He perceives the Bible's unique language, images, form, and style as a divine gift attuned to human needs and human affections. Understanding the baffling, staccato articulation of the human discourse of love, a discourse in which reason is "cut" and words "cannot catch up with the heart," can only shed light on the tribulations of the amorous soul.[58]

The Augustinian father's preoccupation with the Song does not end with his Spanish translation and exposition. He refers abundantly to the Song in the sections devoted to the divine names "Husband" (*Esposo*) and "Beloved" (*Amado*) in his most influential book, *The Names of Christ* (*Los nombres de Cristo*).[59] Fray Luis's work on this book began in prison— as he remarks with a touch of irony in the book's "Dedication," "I must not let this opportunity for leisure go by which the injustice and maliciousness of some people have caused"—but was completed only years later in 1585.[60] While bringing *The Names of Christ* to its final form, Fray Luis also wrote Latin commentaries on the Song (1580 and 1589), based on his earlier Spanish commentary, titled *In Cantica Canticorum Salomonis* (*Commentary on the Song of Solomon*).[61]

Different worlds intersect in Fray Luis: the monastic, mystical, and theological, as well as the new world of humanism and scholarship. Thus his interest in the literal sense of the Song is indebted not only to the mystical literalism of Bernard and Teresa (and possibly the Zohar) but also to a new academic framework in which the meticulous exploration of linguistic and literary phenomena is perceived as vital to acquiring true knowledge. He is the only one of our monastic exegetes who knew Hebrew and insisted on basing his arguments on the nuances of the original Hebrew text, and he is the only one who was committed both to the monastic sphere and to scholarly endeavors. Some two hundred years before biblical criticism came to be celebrated as a major accomplishment of European Enlightenment, the Augustinian Hebraist was exploring the Song with intellectual passion at

Salamanca. J. G. Herder, the renowned eighteenth-century German thinker and biblical critic, was probably unaware of his Spanish precursor, but Fray Luis's translation and commentaries on the Song anticipate Herder's work on the ancient love poem and the Herderian insistence on intellectual freedom and integrity. On returning to teach at Salamanca in 1576 after being acquitted by the Inquisition, Luis de León, the audacious monastic humanist of the Spanish Renaissance, began his first lecture with the memorable words *Dicebamus histerna die*—"We were saying yesterday." With but three words, the Inquisition's persecution is effaced as a meaningless episode that cannot possibly interrupt the ongoing search for truth.

Modern Scholars and the Quest for the Literal Song

From J. G. Herder to Phyllis Trible

The eighteenth century saw the forging of a new literal Song by various scholars across Protestant Europe. It is no coincidence that literalist readings of the Song burst out in Protestant cultures. The Reformation's heightened concern for textual accuracy and the plain sense of Scripture, *sola scriptura*, paved the way for this exegetical revolution. Already Luther had endorsed a pronounced anti-allegorical line in opposition to longstanding Catholic interpretive practices. But whereas Luther could not avoid the allegorical lure in the case of the Song (a purely literal reading would have been too sacrilegious in sixteenth-century Germany) and interpreted it as a political allegory glorifying Solomon's rule under the guidance of the Most High, some of his scholarly descendants did not hesitate to take the Lutheran anti-allegorical stance a step further. By the Age of Enlightenment, the Song was often construed as a grand poem of earthly love that had nothing whatsoever to do with the theological realms of divine love.

We change settings in this chapter, shifting from the world of religious leaders—of rabbis, church fathers, kabbalists, friars, and nuns—to the academic habitat of modern scholars. Indeed, since the eighteenth century, some of the most intriguing and influential shifts in the exegetical history of the Song have taken place in academic circles. This scholarly world has by no means been homogeneous. The perception of the literal Song changes over time and varies widely across disciplines. Fathoming earthly love turns out to be no less demanding than probing divine love. The question of what kind of human love is depicted in the Song has generated different answers, much as the Song's foregrounding of the body has been perceived in astonishingly different ways. Some scholars see the ancient lovers as remarkably chaste, others regard the Song as a collection of wedding songs, and still others find in it an uninhibited celebration of sexuality with no trace of nuptial commitment.

And yet, within this marked scholarly turn to the literal, there are curious pockets of allegory. Though modern scholarship has primarily contributed to the literalist reading of the Song, it has also produced a plethora of highly innovative allegories. Often the lingering presence of allegory is unaccounted for. But, on occasion, we'll consider scholars who deliberately reintroduce allegory into the picture, resisting the modern tendency to cast human and divine love as separate spheres that have nothing in common.

Herder's Literalist Aesthetics

There were various advocates of the literalist Song in eighteenth-century Germany, but Johann Gottfried Herder (1744–1803) was undoubtedly the most fervent and famous of them. In his *Lieder der Liebe* (1778)—a German translation of the Song and a verse-by-verse commentary—he bluntly attacks traditional allegorical readings of the ancient love poem.[1] After centuries of distorted readings, he writes, the time has come to admit the obvious: "What then is the content? What does it treat from beginning to end? . . . *Love, love.* It is simply . . . what it is and with every word suggests: a love song."[2] The literal character of the poem, its original meaning, Herder argues, was obfuscated by Jewish and Christian exegesis and concealed by mystical allegories of divine love. "I read the book and can find in it not the tiniest sign, not the smallest hint that any other meaning is . . . the purpose of the book."[3]

Herder's stance is not as anticlerical as his pronouncements may suggest. His literalist approach is inextricably connected to an endorsement of the Bible's earthly love song as an aesthetic touchstone. Like other scholars of the Enlightenment, Herder sought to rejuvenate the Bible by transforming it from a book justified by theology to a book justified by culture. Although the Enlightenment, as Jonathan Sheehan puts it, "has long symbolized the corrosive effects of modernity on religion . . . the Bible survived, even thrived in this cradle of ostensible secularization," becoming "one of the sturdiest pillars of Western 'culture.'"[4] For Herder, the primary objective was to reconstitute the Bible's authority in aesthetic terms. He was indeed one of the founding figures of the literary approach to the Bible.[5]

Herder, of course, was not the first to admire the poetic grandeur of the Song. Poets such as Yehuda Ha-Levi and John of the Cross had relished the Song as a poetic touchstone long before Herder, and even exegetes such as Bernard and the writers of the Zohar (who were not, strictly speaking, poets) praised its supreme artfulness. Yet none of these precursors sought to define the Song's beauty within an entirely literalist framework. Nor were any of them informed, as Herder was, by modern methodologies drawn from the burgeoning fields of aesthetics, biblical criticism, literary criticism, philology, and ethnography.

Aesthetic explorations of the Song lead Herder to reconsider two traditional presuppositions regarding its dating and authorship. Whereas traditional commentators never question Solomon's authorship under the auspices of divine inspiration, Herder cannot accept this assumption. Judging by the "taste, love, lushness and ornamentation" of the Song, he surmises that it was written during the bountiful, peaceful reign of

Solomon, but—and this is where his account becomes provocative—not by the king himself.[6] In place of Solomon, he positions the anonymous Hebrew folk as the authors of this remarkable ancient poetry. While Solomon may have instigated the Song, it primarily bears the mark of the *Volk*.

Folk poetry (*Volkslied*, "folksong"), which gives voice to the living experiences of common people, is the kind of poetry Herder celebrates in both *Lieder der Liebe* and his later *The Spirit of Hebrew Poetry* (1782–1783).[7] In their primitive, ancient character and their proximity to the world of the senses and to nature, the songs of Hebrew folk, he claims, are comparable to "the most delicate, sweet-smelling flowers which ever grew upon the earth."[8]

Once the Song becomes exemplary folk poetry, it is no longer cherished for its inscrutability and impenetrability. On the contrary, in Herder's eyes (and ears), the Song needs to be regarded as a poetic epitome because of its "ancient simplicity," its spontaneous celebration of rustic life, and its superb orality. Even the lack of structural coherence in the Song does not pose a problem for him. Rather than construing the abrupt and confusing transitions in the Song as tokens of the tumultuous, mystical pursuits of the amorous soul, Herder defines the Song as a collection of love songs (his title *Lieder der Liebe*, *Songs of Love*, underscores this notion), united as "pearls on one thread" (*Perlen an einer Schnur*) by the overriding theme of love and by the spirit of Solomon's reign.[9]

Back to the Orient: "Become with Shepherds a Shepherd"

Contextualizing the Song's aesthetics for Herder means not only tracing the stamp of the Solomonic era but also leaping back to the Bible's original oriental setting. Herder regards the Song as a product of an unparalleled oriental imagination, a text whose subtle meanings are best understood in light of the culture and customs of the East.[10] His well-known guidelines for readers of the Bible in *Letters Concerning the Study of Theology* (1780–1781) offer a succinct formulation of the *Einfühlung* (empathy/sympathy) required for a better appreciation of the Bible's oriental aesthetics:

> Become with shepherds a shepherd, with a people of the sod a man of the land, with the ancients of the Orient an Easterner, if you wish to relish these writings in the atmosphere of their origin; and be on guard against abstractions of dull, new academic prisons, and even more against all so-called artistry which our social circles force and press on those sacred archetypes of the most ancient days.[11]

In following the oriental nuances of the Song à la Herder, one must learn to "become with shepherds a shepherd," to enter empathetically into the convivial realms of the folk imagination that produced these admirable love songs, to draw nearer to the actual cultural and geographic setting of their composition. In Herder's hands, interpretation is not a technical or critical analysis but rather an empathetic submission to the ancient writer's world, to the atmosphere out of which his work emerged.[12]

Empathy (or sympathy), however, is never merely an affirmation of proximity. It also highlights the distance between contemporary readers and the biblical past.[13] When Herder associates the Song with pastoral culture and poetry he does not rely on European eclogues but rather calls us to attend to the cultural specificity of pastoral life in the East. Metaphors that are utterly strange in Western eyes make perfect sense in their oriental habitat. If the Shulamite compares herself to the black tents of Kedar, Herder notes, it is because shepherd tents in the East are coarse and rough but look beautiful and graceful. They are located close to green pastures and water, thus "refreshing the heart of the wandering thirsty oriental" at their sight.[14] And if the beloved's eyes are likened to doves, it is in accordance with Eastern poetic traditions. Herder bases these observations on accounts of travelers to the Levant that circulated in his day. In depicting Eastern tents, he relies on the eighteenth-century Swedish naturalist Fredrik Hasselquist, and in his discussion of the metaphoric nexus of the Shulamite's dovelike eyes, he cites the French diplomat Laurent d'Arvieux's ethnographic observation: "The greatest beauty of the . . . Oriental woman is in her large, dark, wide and prominent eyes. . . . All their songs refer only to the eyes."[15]

It is rather ironic that for all its fidelity to the Song's original context, Herder's *Lieder der Liebe* is colored by European perceptions of the Orient. And yet we can appreciate his attempt to preserve a delicate balance between a sense of identification with the past and a critical aesthetic-philological acknowledgment of cultural difference. What is more, Herder's understanding of the Song as a feast for the eye and the ear is set against those of his contemporaries who regard the ancient Hebrew poetry as "barbaric," replete with jarring guttural sounds (in *The Spirit of Hebrew Poetry*, he dramatizes the dispute through a dialogue between an admirer of ancient Hebrew poetry and one who ridicules it as lacking aesthetic value). We may be more aware today of the imprint of the present on our pursuits of the past (although this awareness may not necessarily curb our tendency to project), but in our attention to cultural specificity and historical perspective and in our attempt to be more open toward other cultures we are in Herder's debt.

The Question of Chastity

The spirit of Herder's age is also apparent in his insistence on the chastity of the Song's lovers. The biblical lovers are viewed via the prism of eighteenth-century models: they are so innocent and virginal that occasionally they even sing lullabies to each other. That Herder was a Lutheran pastor in addition to a prominent scholar may have augmented his need to adhere to contemporary norms of proper sexual conduct.

In construing the Song's love as emblematically innocent, Herder aims to counter the claims of his opponents. One of his goals in publishing his translation of and commentary on the Song in 1778 was to refute rival literalist readings in which the Song was associated with oriental harem songs. The greatest target of his outrage was Johann David Michaelis—a distinguished eighteenth-century German Hebraist—who omitted the Song from his German translation of the Bible, seeing in its secular, erotic verses no mark of sanctity. To doubt the canonicity and chastity of the Song was unthinkable for Herder. He insists on preserving the Song in the canon as an exquisite expression of the most refined human love. That human love, rather than divine love, is celebrated in the Song does not make it less sacred. The Song counts as divine precisely because of its humanity, a humanity that characterizes the Bible as a whole.[16]

Herder's critique of Michaelis and his followers is particularly sharp in his commentary on Song 2:4: "He has brought me to the house of wine / and his banner over me is love." With his typical verve, Herder exclaims: "Oh, morality of the Orient! Oh, propriety! Oh, love! Were the Orientals acquainted with fleshly love? . . . And would a song of love, such as the one we have here, sing of such a thing? . . . The banner of love is nothing more than the image of the tree." [17] Not every oriental scene found in the Song is apparently worth entering. An appreciation of the Song's aesthetic power depends on an empathetic

FIGURE 5. Ephraim Moses Lilien (b. Galicia 1874–1925),
illustration from the Song of Songs, in *Die Bücher der Bible*, 1909.
A Herderian rendition of the Shulamite as a chaste shepherdess.
Courtesy of the Israel Museum.

embrace that explores the naïveté of Eastern shepherds rather than harem life. Though Herder finds no
overt sexuality in the Song, he is well attuned to the
sensuality of its amorous discourse and to the dreamlike, blurred distinctions between the figurative and

literal: "The tree, the fruit and the lover," he writes, "merge into one."[18]

National Revival: The Spirit of the People

Herder's desire to preserve the propriety of the love expressed in the Song is all the more urgent because of his national goals. He sets biblical poetry, the poetry of the ancient Hebrew nation, on a pedestal as superior to the polished, sophisticated poetry that was written in Germany in his time: "The more primitive, i.e. the more vivacious and uninhibited a nation is . . . the more primitively, vivaciously, freely, sensually, lyrically active must its songs be, if indeed it has songs!"[19] It is precisely this kind of vivaciously sensual, ancient national creativity that German culture needs to adopt, Herder proclaims, if it has any aspirations for revival. "If only we could first fully *explain* their poetry on the basis of their national history; and thereupon begin to translate and emulate!"[20]

The Song for Herder thus becomes not only a treasure of the past to be relished on its own terms but also the basis for a new communal love in eighteenth-century Germany. If historical-allegorical exegetes—both Jewish and Christian—used the Song as a founding text by which to define their respective communities, Herder calls for the embrace of biblical poetry to advance a cultural renaissance within the German context. As the product of a superb ancient folk culture, no poetry could be more instrumental than the Song in inspiring a renewed sense of national love among German folk.[21]

Loving one's nation, we should note, is not a biblical concept. In the biblical text, it is the love of God that matters: "And you shall love the Lord your God with all your heart and with all your being and with all your might" (Deut. 6:5). Accordingly, the Promised Land is a token of God's love, not quite an object of love in its own right. In casting the Song as an inspiration for German folk, Herder thus introduces modern perceptions of nationalism into the exegetical history of the Song, creating a new mode of national allegory.

Herder had a tremendous impact on many generations of biblical scholars both in Germany and elsewhere. As a founding figure of many new disciplines his influence can be traced in a variety of scholarly studies on the Song, from the ethnographic to the literary. And given his interest in national revival, his writings on the Song also had a ripple effect in broader cultural settings in which the Song played a role in shaping national identities.

J. G. Wetzstein's *Wasf*: Biblical Ethnographies

Herder never set foot in the Levant, but some of his nineteenth-century followers sought to substantiate his literalist line and interest in Hebrew folklore through

ethnographic fieldwork in the Orient. The most renowned ethnographer of the Song was J. G. Wetzstein
(1815–1905), an orientalist who served as the Prussian
consul in Damascus. In the course of the many years he
spent in Syria, he conducted a study of the wedding customs and songs of Syrian peasants and used his findings
to rethink certain features of the Song.

Centuries earlier, the church father Origen had defined the ancient love poem as a nuptial song, and
many Christian mystics endorsed his definition. But
Wetzstein's interpretation does not aim to reveal spiritual weddings between the Church or the Soul and
Christ. Stripping off allegorical layers of interpretation, he views the Song as a collection of wedding
songs sung in the context of celebrations of entirely
earthly bonds. Relying on the orientalist presupposition that the East had remained unchanged since antiquity, Wetzstein regards the close study of contemporary Syrian weddings as vital to an understanding of
the biblical nuptial ceremonies depicted in the Song.
He points especially to the importance of the threshing board as a pivotal component of Syrian weddings.[22]
During the so-called "royal week," the bride and the
groom are treated as king and queen and seated on a
decorated threshing board, as if it were their throne.
Wetzstein states that there is no symbolic meaning to
this secondary use of a threshing device. Furniture is
rare among Syrian peasants, and thus any board necessarily fulfills several functions.

In calling attention to the staging of peasants' weddings as regal, Wetzstein sets out to solve one of the hermeneutic riddles of the Song: How can the lover be both a shepherd and a king? In Wetzstein's view, the performative aspects of Syrian weddings may explain the multiplicity of roles carried out by the lover in the Song. Much as Syrian peasants are treated as royal during their nuptial celebrations, so too can the biblical lover be a shepherd who plays the role of king on his wedding day. Even if we find it difficult to accept Wetzstein's ethnographic findings today, his inquiries shed light on the folkloric dimension of the Song and its performative playfulness. One of the most captivating features of the Song is indeed the abundance of roles in which the lovers cast themselves and each other: the lover can be a king, a shepherd, and a stag all at once, while the Shulamite can be a shepherdess, a rose, the moon, and the sun.

Wetzstein's reading is most famous for his comparison between the *wasf*, a song of praise performed at Syrian weddings, and the laudatory descriptions of the lovers in the Song.[23] Among the highlights of wedding festivities in Syrian villages, Wetzstein recounts, is the bride's dance (during which she exhibits her fine jewelry) and a group dance, the *debka*, performed in honor of the young couple. The dancing is accompanied by the singing of a *wasf* that portrays the beauty and perfection of the newlyweds, praising every part of their bodies with lavish imagery. Thanks to his knowledge of Arabic and familiarity with Arabic literature, Wetzstein cites representative *wasfs* and maps out pertinent linguistic and literary data to substantiate his comparative angle.

While Wetzstein refers to several descriptive passages in the Song as biblical *wasfs*, his most extensive example is the opening sequence of Song 7:

Turn back, turn back, O Shulamite,

    turn back, that we may behold you.

—Why should you behold the Shulamite

    in the dance of the double rows?

—How fair your feet in sandals,

    O daughter of a nobleman.

The curves of your thighs like wrought rings,

    the handiwork of a master.

Your navel a crescent bowl,

    let mixed wine never lack!

Your belly a mound of wheat

    hedged about with lilies.

Your two breasts like two fawns,

    twins of a gazelle . . .

Your nose like the tower of Lebanon

    looking out toward Damascus . . .

How fair you are, how sweet,

    O Love, among delights! (1–7)

For Wetzstein, this biblical love song, with its detailed praise of the beloved's body, clearly resembles the *wasfs* he had heard at Syrian village weddings. Similarly, he regards the Shulamite's solo dance and the group dancing in "double rows" as the ancient counterparts of contemporary Syrian wedding dances.[24]

Though Wetzstein does not mention the fact that the Shulamite is hailed here as a *bat-nadiv*, a "daughter of a nobleman," he probably would interpret this designation as further corroboration of his argument regarding the aggrandizing of the rural bride.

The Prussian consul did not write much about the Song, but his ethnographic accounts were a source of inspiration for subsequent ethnographies. Among Wetzstein's notable heirs were the ethnographers G. H. Dalman and S. H. Stephan, who explored parallels to the Song in Palestine during the early twentieth century.[25] Beyond the ethnographic world, the *wasf* has become the standard term for the descriptive sequences of the Song—though laudatory amorous songs and poems can be found, of course, in many other cultural settings, as Shakespeare's sonnet "My Mistress' Eyes Are Nothing Like the Sun" reminds us.

Shlomo Löwisohn's Amorous Triangle: Jewish Enlightenment

The first shock waves of the literalist readings of the Song made their way to the intellectual circles of the Jewish Enlightenment in the late eighteenth and early nineteenth centuries. At this time, a whole gallery of Jewish Enlightenment thinkers and writers were engaged in redefining the Bible for a growing number of modern Jews interested in embracing the fruits of modern scholarship while preserving their Jewish identity.[26]

The scholar and poet Shlomo Löwisohn (1789–1821) provided the most substantive introduction to the literalist-aesthetic reading of the Song within the framework of the Jewish Enlightenment. Born in Hungary, Löwisohn later moved to Vienna, where he published his most renowned book *Melitzat yeshurun* (*The Rhetoric of Israel*) in 1816. Written in flowery biblical Hebrew, *Melitzat yeshurun* includes extensive adaptations of the commentaries of Herder and Robert Lowth (the greatest advocate of the literary Bible in the English Enlightenment) on various biblical texts, the Song of Songs among them.

Löwisohn solves the enigma of the double identity of the lover by splitting it, or, rather, by construing the Song as a passionate, triangular drama involving the Shulamite, the king, and the shepherd. The Shulamite in his rendition prefers her rustic lover to the king. And although King Solomon woos her fervently and forces her to reside in his harem, he does not succeed in preventing the chaste maiden from running off to meet her loved one in the fields time and again. Spurning every royal allurement, the Shulamite ignores Solomon's call for her to return to the harem—"Turn back, turn back, O Shulamite" (Song 7:1)—remaining faithful to her humble shepherd.[27] Löwisohn thus manages to preserve the lovers' chastity in Herderian fashion without omitting harem life from the picture.

While providing a strikingly sensuous dramatization of this amorous triangle, Löwisohn calls upon his readers to consider the Song's poetic grandeur.[28] In keeping with Herder's *Lieder der Liebe*, Löwisohn claims that the similes and metaphors of the Song may seem strange—the beloved's hair could hardly be similar to a flock of sheep—but one needs to bear in mind that the grand biblical artist drew his inspiration from the realities of oriental pastoral life. The shepherd, whose sheep and fields are his entire world, uses everyday experience as a source of figurative language. Envious of the shepherd, even King Solomon occasionally uses pastoral images to lure the Shulamite.[29]

Reading the Song as a triangular drama was a popular exegetical move in nineteenth-century scholarship, both within and beyond Jewish circles. The king–shepherd–Shulamite triangle appears in a range of studies, among them Ernest Renan's *Le Cantique des cantiques* (1860). Both Löwisohn and Renan may have been inspired by an earlier consideration of this triangle in a 1772 work of the Christian exegete J. F. Jacobi. The boundaries between Jewish and Christian commentaries became ever more permeable as the Enlightenment progressed and ended up being even less apparent (though still noticeable) in twentieth-century scholarship. What is far more vital than religious affiliations to modern exegetical mappings are disciplinary and theoretical frameworks.

Franz Rosenzweig's Critique of Literalism

Franz Rosenzweig, the great German-Jewish philosopher of the early twentieth century, offers a fascinating critique of Enlightenment views of the Song in *The*

Star of Redemption (1921). "Up to the threshold of the nineteenth century," Rosenzweig claims, "the Song of Songs was recognized as a love lyric and precisely thereby simultaneously as 'mystical' poem. One simply knew that the I and Thou of human discourse is without more ado also the I and Thou between God and man. One knew that the distinction between immanence and transcendence disappears in language."[30] Not despite the fact that the Song was a "real" love poem (i.e., "worldly") but because of that was it received as a genuine "spiritual" poem regarding human–divine love.

Rosenzweig's comment is meant primarily as a critique of Herder, whose literalist-aesthetic approach to the Song neglects the poem's special position between human and divine love.[31] For Rosenzweig, the Song illustrates a philosophical truth that the poem's secularization laid bare: that before modern times, interpersonal relations necessarily presupposed the "I and Thou" between God and humanity.[32] Rosenzweig provocatively sides with mystical exegetes in his debunking of Herderian presuppositions (he strangely overlooks the theological underpinnings of Herder's commentary), but his goal is not to return to the Middle Ages. Rather, he aspires to redefine the interrelations between human and divine love from a modern perspective, highlighting the blurred demarcation between immanence and transcendence in the Song's amorous discourse while granting an equally elevated position to the mystical and the literal.

Rosenzweig's critique of Wetzstein (though he doesn't mention his name) is even more scathing:

> The hopeless caprice and text-critical adventurousness of all those interpretations into the objective realm of the "musical drama" made the learned spirits receptive to a new view. . . . And then it was suddenly discovered that among the peasants of Syria the wedding is celebrated on the analogy of a royal wedding to this day, with the groom as king and the bride as the royal choice. . . . Now everything is once more enclosed in the lyrical duo-solitude of the lover and the beloved. And now, above all, the simile is brought back into the "most original" sense of the Songs . . . the shepherd who is bridegroom by the king whom he feels himself to be. This, however, is the point at which we are aiming. Love simply cannot be "purely human."[33]

Rosenzweig mocks the Wetzsteinian ethnographic approach for its fanciful, reductive literalism.[34] The "objective realm" that such ethnographers claim to have found in Syrian weddings, the supposedly authentic oriental window to the "most original" historical sense of the Song, is nothing but an "adventurous" tale that ironically ends up decontextualizing the biblical text by overlooking the inseparability of human and divine love. Almost sixty years before the publication of Edward Said's *Orientalism*, Rosenzweig formulated a critical assessment of orientalist methodologies.[35] To be sure, Rosenzweig was not concerned with the political implications of Western projections onto the East, but he was a precursor to Said in laying bare the blind spots of orientalist research.

What makes Rosenzweig's reading particularly gripping is its poetic force and unique attention to literary nuances. He beautifully captures the dreamlike qualities of the Song: "The speech of love is all present: dream and reality, sleep of the limbs and awaking of the heart, intertwine indistinguishably. Everything is equally present, equally fleeting and equally alive."[36] At another point, he calls attention to the singularity of the Song's "I." "Comparatively speaking," Rosenzweig writes, "the word 'I' occurs this frequently in no other book in the Bible. . . . Like a single sustained organ note, it runs under the whole melodic-harmonic texture of mezzo-sopranos and sopranos."[37]

There is something idiosyncratic in Rosenzweig's commentary on the Song and his mode of scholarship. His comments in *The Star of Redemption* did not generate an interpretive trend. Nonetheless, his densely philosophical-poetic reading of the ancient love poem, his singular "sustained organ note" running under "the whole melodic-harmonic texture of mezzo-sopranos," is a notable landmark in the far from linear biography of the Song.

T. J. Meek and the Cultic Approach: Rites and Hymns of the Ancient Near East

Amid the explosion of literal readings emerged a counter perspective, primarily from scholars of the cultic approach. The discovery and decipherment of ancient Mesopotamian texts in the early twentieth century opened up new interpretive possibilities. If nineteenth-century ethnographers read the ancient love poem against the backdrop of Eastern customs, twentieth-century scholars of the cultic approach advanced what they perceived as a more pertinent framework of contextualization: the rites and hymns of the ancient Near East. With the transition from the contemporary Orient to the ancient Near East, allegory, strangely enough, reemerged with a distinct, new look. Under this approach, the Song is no longer perceived as a secular corpus, but rather as a sanctified poetic celebration of divine love whose origins may be traced back to Canaanite fertility rites.

In his work of the 1920s, T. J. Meek, a Bible scholar and archaeologist at the University of Toronto, searched for parallels to the Song in liturgical texts rejoicing in the sacred marriage of the Canaanite divine couple, Ishtar and Tammuz. The following Babylonian hymn (which he translated) is his principal example:

I beheld thee and . . .
Shine out like a star of the sky! . . .
How I long for the abounding one!
The day that the lord of my right hand
embraced me.
Come, take me! I give welcome to the son . . .
How gorgeous she is; how resplendent she is!
She seeketh out the beautiful garden of thy
abundance.

Today my heart is joy (and) gladness.
O, come down to the garden of the king
(which) reeks with cedar.[38]

According to Meek, this hymn was sung in honor of the sacred marriage of Tammuz and Ishtar. It was part of an annual ritual rather than a celebration of a one-time event, for the heavenly bond between the two gods needed to be renewed cyclically: Tammuz was thought to descend to the underworld every winter and then was brought back to life in springtime. As he united with Ishtar on his return, fertility was restored to the land, and the dirges over his death were replaced by hymns of love. Where are the parallels to the Hebrew Song? Among other observations, Meek points to the similarities apparent in the depictions of the amorous gardens and the beloved's search for her loved one.

But why, one may well wonder, should hymns of pagan rites be pertinent to the monotheistic setting of the biblical text? Meek's argument (and this is true of other proponents of this approach) is that the Canaanite traditions were transformed within the Yahweh cult: their polytheistic features were effaced, or rather reinterpreted, to suit monotheistic precepts. Some traces of this cultural translation, however, survived. Thus it comes as no surprise that the Song was incorporated into the liturgy of Passover, a Jewish spring holiday: "The festival and the book belong together because they have always been together."[39]

Meek also calls attention to another remnant of sorts: the appearance of the term *she'ol*, the "underworld," in Song 8:6: "For love is as mighty as death, as strong as Sheol."[40] When *she'ol* is evoked in the Song and elsewhere in the Bible, it is primarily a figure of speech or a synonym for death or the world of the dead (in biblical monotheism, there is no afterlife). Meek, however, revives the term's dormant mythological import, claiming that in its original context, Song 8:6 "was manifestly a reference to the power of the love of the goddess to win the god back from the netherworld."[41] True, Tammuz and Ishtar are not mentioned in the Song, but this does not mean that the ancient Hebrews were unaware of their fervent love against the backdrop of the shadows of death. Ezekiel is Meek's witness, for the wrathful prophet rebukes the women who mourn over Tammuz's death at the Temple gate in Jerusalem (Ezekiel 8:14).

The cultic approach continued to gain recognition in the decades that followed, though Meek's exploration of the Song's Canaanite origin was later replaced by studies of Sumerian parallels. In the 1950s and 1960s, S. N. Kramer published several studies arguing that the divine hymns of Sumer were more relevant to the understanding of the Song than were Canaanite fertility rites.[42] Gradually, the cultic approach waned, as it was criticized for its speculative character. Nonetheless, in calling for a consideration of the Song in relation to the hymns of the ancient Near East and in rescuing Mesopotamian traditions from oblivion, the

FIGURE 6. Lovers Embracing on Bed. Clay plaque. Mesopotamia, 2000–1600 BCE. Such scenes are considered representations of the cult of the sacred marriage. The bearded man holds his beloved's head in the palm of one hand and rests his other hand upon her waist. The long-haired woman encircles her companion's waist with one arm, offering her breast with the other. Photo © RMN-Grand Palais (musée du Louvre) / Hervé Lewandowski / Franck Raux.

cultic-mythological school has added a precious comparative angle to the reading of the Song. In more diffuse ways (and given the fluid boundaries between religious and secular poetry), such exquisite hymns could just as well have served as a source of inspiration for Hebrew poets who were eager to celebrate the pleasures of earthly love.[43]

Robert Alter's Garden of Metaphors: The Literary Approach

Herder's call for a consideration of the aesthetic aspects of the Song was endorsed by subsequent readers. But it was only in the 1980s that this literary turn became a full-fledged academic trend. Then, as now, Robert Alter has been one of the leading figures in advocating a literary approach to the Bible. A professor of Hebrew and comparative literature at the University of California, Berkeley, he published two groundbreaking books in the 1980s—*The Art of Biblical Narrative* (1981) and *The Art of Biblical Poetry* (1985)—in which he introduced twentieth-century methodologies of literary criticism into the study of biblical poetics.

One of the chapters of *The Art of Biblical Poetry*, "The Garden of Metaphor," is devoted to the Song of Songs. Alter's aim is not to recover the historical and geographical life-setting of biblical aesthetics (à la Herder), but rather to explore the Song's poetics as defined in the text itself while comparing it to other modes of biblical poetry. That the imagery of the Song is a curious mixture of pastoral, urban, and regal metaphors, he argues, leaves "scant grounds for concluding whether the poems were composed among shepherds or courtiers or somewhere in between."[44] There is something so untypical about the Song's poetics that it escapes any decisive classification. The Book of Job and Proverbs may be attributed to literary elites and Psalms to priestly circles, but it "is only in the Song of Songs that there is no one giving instruction or exhortation, no leader or hierophant, no memorializer of national experience, but instead the voices of two lovers praising each other, yearning for each other, proffering invitations to enjoy." Whether or not these secular love songs were composed by folk poets, Alter goes on to suggest, "it is clear that their poetic idiom is one that, for all its artistic sophistication, is splendidly accessible to the folk."[45]

Alter turns to no Syrian rural weddings or Mesopotamian sacred marriage rites (he is critical of both the ethnographic and cultic approaches) but rather leads us into the intricacies of the literary world of the poem. Thus, his close reading of the series of interrelated metaphors and similes in Song 7 (Wetzstein's *wasf*) begins with a broader consideration of its figurative scope, highlighting the ways in which the poem moves rapidly, with no concern for unity, from artistry to agriculture and then from the animal kingdom to architectural splendors. He construes the choice to begin with a comparison between the beloved's thighs and the artisan's handiwork as a self-reflexive comment on the

Song's poetic finesse, an "implied celebration of arti-fice." In the following lines (Song 7:3–5), the gaze shifts to the beloved's wheatlike belly surrounded by lilies, superimposing "an agricultural image on an erotic one."[46] The flamboyant elaboration of the metaphoric frame does not diminish the eroticism of the scene. On the contrary, it generates a delightfully witty series of double entendres by which to marvel, with decorum, at the enticing body parts of the dancing Shulamite. Alter detects a similar ingenious use of erotic figuration in the vertical description of the male body in Song 5:10–16. In this, he is very far, of course, from Herder's per-ception of the Song as a poetic homage to chaste love.

Alter ends his meanderings in the garden of amo-rous metaphors with a passionate salute to the unique literalism of the Song: "Only in the Song of Songs ... is the writer's art directed to the imaginative realiza-tion of a world of uninhibited self-delighting play, without moral conflict, without the urgent context of history and nationhood and destiny, without the looming perspectives of a theological world-view."[47] His reading remains one of the highlights of literalist readings of the Song.

Phyllis Trible's Depatriarchalized Song: Feminist Perspectives

There is one more mode of literalism that has had a major impact in twentieth-century scholarship:

feminist criticism. The founding figure in this realm is the feminist biblical scholar Phyllis Trible, who taught at the Union Theological Seminary in New York. In 1973, Trible published a highly influential article titled "Depatriarchalizing in Biblical Interpretation" in which she challenges the sexist presuppositions of traditional commentators and calls attention to the more liberating gender clues in the biblical text that had heretofore been ignored.[48] To be more precise, she offers a critique of both sexist and early feminist approaches to Scripture. What previous readers neglected to take into account, she claims, is that patriarchy does not have "God on its side." The women's movement thus "errs when it dismisses the Bible as inconsequential or condemns it as enslaving. In rejecting Scripture women ironically accept male chauvinistic interpretations and thereby capitulate to the very view they are protesting."[49]

The Song of Songs is one of Trible's prime examples for a depatriarchalized text within the biblical corpus. Trible first extols the ancient love poem's unique representation of gender roles in "Depatriarchalizing in Biblical Interpretation" but provides a more extensive reading in *God and the Rhetoric of Sexuality* (1978). In a chapter titled "Love's Lyrics Redeemed," she construes the Song as an uplifting "garden of Eros" where the patriarchal configurations of gender established with the expulsion from the Garden of Eden are utterly undone. If the woman's curse in Eden relegates her to a subordinate position—"Your desire shall be for your man, but he shall rule over you" (Genesis 3:16)—in the Song's amorous gardens, where love is harmonious and sexuality is unabashedly celebrated, the beloved can declare: "I am my lover's and for me is his desire" (7:10).[50]

In Trible's Song, "there is no male dominance, no female subordination, and no stereotyping of either sex."[51] And in this world that defies the connotations of "second sex," the woman's voice can be dominant—so much so that she is the one to open and close the amorous dialogues. The emphasis on feminine perspectives is further enhanced by the ongoing presence of the daughters of Jerusalem, as well as by the various references to the mothers of the lovers (the fathers are never mentioned). What is more, there is a recurrent use of the unusual term "mother's house."[52] Elsewhere in the Bible, the father's house prevails, but in the Song the maternal abode is the treasured site to which the beloved wishes to bring her lover (Song 3:4, 8:2).

Although Trible endorses a pronounced literalist position, her reading is not innocent of allegorical underpinnings. She presents the Song's love lyrics as a redemptive correction to the original narrative of the "fall" of woman in the Garden of Eden. Accordingly, the Shulamite becomes a "second Eve" of sorts who takes part in creating a redeeming garden of love. Trible's reading has been criticized both for its theological bent and for its idealization. Here, as elsewhere, she overlooks the Bible's patriarchal stamp: the vigilant brothers and violent guards don't really share the lovers' experience of love as the ultimate equalizer.[53]

Despite these criticisms, Trible's reading has left an indelible mark on contemporary readings of the Song. The invitation to "depatriarchalize" the ancient love poem has set in relief the refreshingly egalitarian construction of love in the Song, features that, we may assume, compelled female readers in earlier periods as well (Teresa and her nuns are but one notable example). In Trible's wake, the Song has become one of the privileged texts of feminist criticism. In fact, the editor of the *Feminist Companion to the Bible*—Athalya Brenner—chose to devote two volumes to feminist readings of the Song (1993, 2000) in light of its centrality.[54]

Julia Kristeva: The Dynamic of Absence in the Discourse of Love

The final figure in our consideration of the scholarly reception of the Song is Julia Kristeva, a Bulgarian-French philosopher, literary critic, psychoanalyst, and feminist who devotes one of the richest chapters of her *Tales of Love* (1983), titled "A Holy Madness: She and He," to the Song. Written only a few years after Trible's *God and the Rhetoric of Sexuality*, Kristeva's reading of the Song follows a decidedly different feminist route. Kristeva focuses not on gender equality and social norms, but rather on the Shulamite's singular language and subjectivity. By "her lyrical, dancing, theatrical language," the Shulamite becomes a "prototype of the modern individual," a woman who acquires sovereignty "through her love and the discourse that causes it to be."[55] Kristeva's greatest departure from Trible is evident in her consideration of the darker shades of love. Her Shulamite is not an advocate of amorous harmony, but rather "limpid, intense, divided, quick, upright, suffering, hoping," a woman "who on account of her love, becomes the first Subject in the modern sense of the term. Divided. Sick and yet sovereign."[56] The dominance of the Shulamite's voice is thus inseparable from her capacity to experience and express most forcefully the tumultuous intensity of the diverse split aspects of love.

Feminism is by no means Kristeva's only theoretical prism. Her reading is also informed by literary theory, linguistics, and psychoanalysis. With this interdisciplinary entourage she offers a reconsideration of the literal-allegorical debate. Although she accepts the assumption that the Song was initially secular, she is primarily interested in the ways in which it lends itself to allegorical readings. The Song is most appropriate for explorations of divine love in her account because of its attentiveness to the intricate tensions between presence and absence, between desire for fulfillment and an equally forceful desire for elusive, unfulfilled love. The human lover, like his divine counterpart, paradoxically exists, is sensed intensely, but at the same time "hastes away."[57]

To highlight the pivotal role of disappearances and splits in the realm of love—whether human or divine—Kristeva adopts Renan's version of the splitting of the lover between King Solomon and the shepherd. The advantage of such splitting, according to Kristeva, is that it underscores the tension between "a present (incarnate) loved one, who would be the shepherd, and another nonrepresentable one, holder of authority and taboo, forever out of reach although he conditions the lover's existence, and who is God (here, Solomon)."[58] God (or Solomon) is thus positioned as the unreachable holder of paternal authority in a triangular drama of an Oedipal bent. He is not quite the actual lover, but the one whose absence is a prerequisite for love.

Kristeva's foregrounding of absence in the Song is inextricably connected to her understanding of the evasiveness of the amorous discourse and its heavy reliance on metaphors. "Love," writes Kristeva, "is undisputably the privileged experience for the blossoming of metaphor," for the amatory figure of speech discloses uncertainty concerning the bond and an ongoing preoccupation with the limits of language.[59] The transference of meaning via metaphor (the Greek term *metaphorá* means "to transport") represents, as it were, the lover's attempt to transfer to the place of the other. Such transferences, however, are far from smooth. The amorous discourse interrupts the "normal, univocal exchange of information. . . . [E]ach bit of information is loaded with semantic polyvalence and thus becomes undecidable connotation."[60] The metaphoric designation of the lover's name as "an oil poured out" in the opening chapter of the Song is thus exemplary:

The "name" that is evoked almost from the very beginning induces intoxication; its precision and uniqueness trigger, it would seem, an overflowing of meaning, a flow of significations and sensations comparable to that produced by caresses, perfumes and oils.... [T]he body and the name, are thus not only placed on the same level but fused in the same logic of undecidable infinitization, semantic polyvalence brewed by the state of love.[61]

Kristeva's dense, poetic writing and juggling of literal and allegorical readings alongside several theoretical lines of inquiry are not easy to follow. But her casting of the Song in a world of uncertainties accentuates in unprecedented ways the fissures and splits in the ancient discourse of love. In her insistence on the complication of signification in the Song, Kristeva is closer to Bernard or Teresa than to Herder. Finding no "ancient simplicity" in the Song, she celebrates its "undecidable infinitization." But in Kristeva's reading, the riddling qualities of the Song sound decisively different, as they are set within the contours of postmodern theory.[62] For some readers, Kristeva may seem to keep too close to allegorical zones, but her provocative refusal to discard allegory as relevant to the reading of the Song serves as a vital invitation to reconsider the interrelations between the representations of human and divine love.[63]

We have followed the twists and turns in the history of the scholarly reception of the Song from the

Enlightenment to the twentieth century. Regardless of pronounced differences among them, all these scholars introduce the Song into the world of modern humanistic inquiry. They all rely on the underlying notion that a deeper understanding of our cultural heritage is a prerequisite for a better understanding of humanity; they are all concerned with redefining the means by which we reflect on human experiences and creativity; they all strive to breathe new life into the ancient love poem, making it meaningful for a modern age.

Though adamantly intellectual, this world of inquiry by no means lacks passion. Modern scholars turn out to be no less avid readers of the Song than the rabbis and monks who preceded them. Indeed, some of the most passionate readers of the Song are scholars. Herder, who invites us to become "shepherds with shepherds" and to plunge into the rustic lives of the biblical lovers, expresses this passion most overtly. But in all of the subsequent studies we considered (with the exception, perhaps, of Wetzstein's ethnographic research) one can find a profound admiration for the Song's grandeur—from praises of the ancient love poem as a poetic epitome and an exquisite garden of metaphors to celebrations of its unique egalitarian spirit and take on gender.

Scholars may seem to roam in secluded worlds, but their studies are informed not only by changing intellectual climates but also by broader cultural contexts. Herder's literary Bible is inseparable from his vision of German renaissance, Löwisohn strives to fashion a

Song in the spirit of the Jewish Enlightenment, and Trible writes against the backdrop of the rise of the feminist movement. What is more, scholarly writings often find their way—whether directly or by circuitous paths—far beyond academic circles. In the next chapter, we will explore the spread of Herder's *Lieder der Liebe* and the vast reach of the Song itself within American literature and culture.

Song of America

From Walt Whitman to Toni Morrison

When the Puritans arrived on the shores of America in the seventeenth century, the Song of Songs was not among the biblical texts that they projected onto the new landscapes. Verses from Exodus, Deuteronomy, the Prophets, and the New Testament were far more vital to the fashioning of their errand in the new Promised Land.[1] It took more than two hundred years before the ancient love poem acquired a quintessentially American look. The Song's greatest American readers were modern writers and poets of the nineteenth and twentieth centuries for whom the very fact that the Song was not colored by Puritan visions made it all the more enticing as a springboard for a radical reimagining of American dreams as well as a redefining of love and literature.

The protagonists of this chapter are three of America's literary giants: Walt Whitman, Herman Melville, and Toni Morrison. Their work offers some of the most intriguing modern experiments with the Song. All three advance new literal readings of the Song while refusing to relinquish allegory, all three insist on dismantling the traditional elevation of the soul over the body and the allegorical over the literal, all three experiment with new definitions of love, all three refrain from focusing solely on heterosexual love, all three cross the boundaries between poetry and prose, and all three use the Song to rethink foundational moments in American history.

We've already noted earlier moments in the nuanced history of the literary reception of the Song—from medieval Hebrew poetry to the "Spiritual Canticle" of John of the Cross. In modern contexts, literature assumes a more pronounced exegetical role. This shift may be attributed to the diminishing role of theological exegesis, but it is also indebted to the growing scholarly acknowledgment of the aesthetic features of the biblical text from the Enlightenment onward. Once the Bible is defined less as revealed truth than as grand literature, poets and writers can, more than ever before, regard themselves as suitable (if not the most suitable) exegetes.[2] Literary exegetes are not interested in systematic interpretations. More often than not, they do not even admit explicitly that they are evoking biblical verses or relying on other commentaries. To top it all, they never hesitate to recast biblical scenes in contemporary contexts. But the poetic license of writers does not make their exegetical endeavors less earnest or pertinent. Quite the contrary, literary flights of the imagination—despite and, at times, because of their radical departures from the biblical text—may give rise to interpretive insights available to no other exegetical mode.

Whitman's "Song of Myself"

The first edition of *Leaves of Grass*, published in 1855, sold poorly. Some of its early readers were sympathetic, but most were bewildered by its sexual frankness. A particularly enraged reviewer defined Whitman's work as nothing but a "mass of stupid filth."[3] This resentment did not subside with the publication of subsequent editions (Whitman rewrote the book obsessively throughout his life and published several editions, culminating in the 1891–1892 "deathbed edition"). In 1865 Whitman was fired from his job at the Department of the Interior when a working copy of *Leaves of Grass* was found on his desk. Later, in 1882, Boston district attorney Oliver Stevens wrote a letter to Whitman's publisher, James R. Osgood, condemning *Leaves of Grass* as obscene literature. "Song of Myself" was among the poems whose removal was requested. Osgood did not want to risk his reputation and demanded revisions. Instead of complying with Osgood's request, Whitman managed to find a new publisher: Rees Welsh & Company. He was right in assuming that the controversy would only increase sales.[4] The first printing of this new edition was released on July 18, 1882, and sold out in a day. Over time, *Leaves of Grass* became part and parcel of the literary canon, with "Song of Myself" often considered its crowning poetic feat.

Whitman's "Song of Myself" strives to be nothing less than the ultimate Song, a grand Song of all possible loves: the love of the self, the love of others, the love of the body, the love of the soul, and the love of America. Whitman does not evoke the Song of Songs explicitly in "Song of Myself," but his debt to the ancient love poem is above all apparent in the title, which calls to mind the superlative title of "Song of Songs," and in his quest for poetic epitome within the realm of love.[5]

Beyond these primary links, there are sections of "Song of Myself" where the dialogue with the ancient love poem is particularly palpable. One such moment is the renowned opening:

> I celebrate myself, and sing myself,
> And what I assume you shall assume,
> For every atom belonging to me as good belongs to you.
>
> I loafe and invite my soul,
> I lean and loafe at my ease observing a spear of summer
>   grass.
> My tongue, every atom of my blood, form'd from this
>   soil, this air . . .
>
> Houses and rooms are full of perfumes, the shelves are
>   crowded with perfumes,
> I breathe the fragrance myself and know it and like it,
> The distillation would intoxicate me also, but I shall not
>   let it.

The atmosphere is not a perfume, it has no taste of the
    distillation, it is odorless,
It is for my mouth forever, I am in love with it,
I will go to the bank by the wood and become
    undisguised and naked,
I am mad for it to be in contact with me.

The smoke of my own breath,
Echoes, ripples, buzz'd whispers, love-root, silk-thread,
    crotch and vine,
My respiration and inspiration, the beating of my heart,
    the passing of blood and air through my lungs . . .
A few light kisses, a few embraces, a reaching around of
    arms . . .
The feeling of health, the full-noon trill, the song of me
    rising from bed and meeting the sun. (1–2: 1–28)[6]

Whitman opens his poem with a conventional iambic
pentameter line, as if adhering to the model of classical
epics, but then abandons metrics for a free-flowing line
that responds to the ever-shifting play of the senses.
Free verse is Whitman's claim to fame and most renowned stylistic innovation. Interestingly, this grand
poetic feat and major break with European poetic conventions is inspired by biblical poetry, where one finds
no meter or rhyme.[7] To accentuate the biblical touch,
Whitman casts some of his opening lines in the mold
of parallelism, the formal organizing principle of biblical poetry. "I celebrate myself, and sing myself" is the
majestic opening parallelism. Other parallelisms appear in subsequent lines.

Of all biblical poems, the Song has a distinct resonance: the jubilant voice of a poet in love and the welter
of senses in "rooms full of perfumes" or "along the fields"
disclose a special affinity with the sensual exuberance of
the ancient love poem.[8] No one before Whitman had
captured the sense of joy of the biblical lovers' savoring
of bodily pleasures and the freshness of their verdant
bed. No one before him had reproduced the wild,
dreamy pace of the invitations to go out into the fields.
No one before him had reveled in the Song's celebration
of human love and sexuality with such bravura.

Whitman wants to invent a new kind of American
Bible, one that no Puritan could have dreamed of. To
be sure, he doesn't hesitate to juggle biblical texts that
were cherished in the Puritan exegetical world—be
they Psalms or the Prophets—inverting them in diverse ways. But he must have felt a particular joy in
placing at the very center of his poetry a biblical song
whose affirmation of love and the body had played no
crucial role in the austere lives of the founding figures
of American culture.

In repositioning the Song in this fashion, Whitman
was indebted in part to the growing impact of Herder's
writings within American academic circles. It took a
while for Herder's new literalist readings of the Song
to cross the Atlantic, but by the mid-nineteenth century they had been adopted by American academics.
The most notable proponent of Herder's approach was
George R. Noyes, a professor of Hebrew at Harvard,
who published a new annotated translation of the

Song of Songs in 1846 that fully endorsed the continental literalist-aesthetic approach.[9] Knowing no German, Whitman could not have read *Lieder der Liebe* directly, but he was familiar with the work of Noyes and possibly with that of some of Herder's other American followers.[10]

Whitman shares Herder's perception of the Song as a grand aesthetic touchstone and is as committed to highlighting the literal dimension of the Song. His sole explicit reference to Herder at the very end of "A Backward Glance O'er Travel'd Roads" (1888) indicates that he was aware of the contours of the Herderian perspective on the Song: "Concluding with two items for the imaginative genius of the West, when it worthily rises—First, what Herder taught to the young Goethe, that really great poetry is always (like the Homeric or Biblical canticles) the result of a national spirit, and not the privilege of a polish'd and select few; Second, that the strongest and sweetest songs yet remain to be sung."[11] And yet there are distinct differences. For Whitman, Herder's admiration for the lovers' chastity has no appeal. Herder's adherence to chaste models of love may have seemed far better than the Puritan denial of the body, but they were still irrelevant to a reading of the Song. Whitman's Song is an unbound Song, one in which the eroticism of the ancient love poem is magnified beyond inhibition.

What is more, Whitman experiments with modes of human love that are not quite part of the amorous discourse of the Song. The celebration of self-love is one of the most pronounced swerves in Whitman's Song. His notions of the self, and all the more so of self-love, are unmistakably modern concepts. The Shulamite and her lover are not preoccupied with their own naked bodies or their own tongues and breath, nor do they sniff their own armpits with pleasure ("the scent of these arm-pits aroma finer than prayer," *Song of Myself* 24:524), though we do find rare moments of self-celebration in the Song. With an uncommon use of the word "I," the Shulamite occasionally ventures to celebrate her own beauty in statements such as: "I am black but comely," "I am a lily of Sharon, Rose of the valley," and "I am a wall, and my breasts like towers."[12]

Another notable departure is evident in the gender fluidity of Whitman's Song. Whereas the ancient love poem revolves around heterosexual love, Whitman's "you" encompasses both male and female (something that is impossible in the grammatically gendered Hebrew), adding a homoerotic potentiality to the multiple loves that intersect in "Song of Myself."

The Poet of the Body and the Poet of the Soul

Whitman is by no means solely an advocate of earthly love. In a cryptic note on *Leaves of Grass*, he wonders about the title of his collection: "What name? Religious canticles. These ought to be the *brain and the living spirit* (elusive, indescribable, indefinite)."[13] Of course Whitman did not actually use "religious canticles" as a title for the poems of *Leaves of Grass.* Such a title would have been not only too bland but also misleading. Whitman's religious imaginings, after all, entail an anticlerical, iconoclastic dismantling of traditional configurations of faith.

Designating himself in "Song of Myself" as "the poet of the body and the poet of the soul," Whitman is keen on fashioning a reading of the biblical canticles that is both literal and allegorical. In another well-known moment of the poem, he turns to an addressee who is a cross between his soul and a divinely human or humanly divine lover.

> I believe in you my soul, the other I am must not abase itself to you,
> And you must not be abased to the other.
> Loafe with me on the grass, loose the stop from your throat,
> Not words, not music or rhyme I want, not custom or lecture, not even the best,
> Only the lull I like, the hum of your valved voice.
>
> I mind how once we lay such a transparent summer morning,
> How you settled your head athwart my hips and gently turn'd over upon me,
> And parted the shirt from my bosom-bone, and plunged your tongue to my bare-stript heart,
> And reach'd till you felt my beard, and reach'd till you held my feet . . .

And I know that the hand of God is the promise of
    my own,
And I know that the spirit of God is the brother of
    my own,
And that all the men ever born are also my brothers, and
    the women my sisters and lovers,
And that a kelson of the creation is love . . . (5:82–95)

Mystical readings of the Song—from the Zohar to
Santa Teresa's *Meditations*—can be highly erotic, as
we have seen, but in Whitman's poem, the sexual dimension of spiritual love is blasphemously intensified.
Whitman does not hesitate to lower God to the level
of grass and "loaf" with his soul or his divine-human
lover. And in a moment of sheer ecstasy, the lover in
turn ventures to part "the shirt from [his] bosom-
bone" and plunge his tongue into the speaker's "bare-
stript heart." The blurring of the boundaries between
earthly and heavenly love is accompanied by the liter-
alization of the stock metaphor of the "hand of God."
God's hand becomes flesh, taking part in a distinctly
erotic love scene, a provocative elaboration of the
verse: "His left hand is under my head, and his right
hand doth embrace me" (Song 2:6). Santa Teresa
could have probably recognized a certain similarity
between her mystical encounter with the angel and
Whitman's ecstatic experience on that memorable
summer morning. She could possibly even have recognized the relevance of gender fluidity to such magical

moments but would have been appalled, we may assume, by the utter conflation of body and soul, by the radical humanization of God, and by the Romantic deification of the poet.

What makes Whitman's mystical reading of the Song all the more heretical is the fact that it does not privilege Christianity. The Whitmanian soul bears the mark of various creeds, from Christian spirituality to Hinduism. Deeply influenced by Emerson's Transcendentalism and concept of the "Over-Soul," Whitman refuses to regard any religion whatsoever as the ultimate answer to the human spiritual quest and is suspicious of all modes of institutional faith.[14] Elsewhere in "Song of Myself," in Section 41, he juggles several religions and gods at once:

> Magnifying and applying come I,
> Outbidding at the start the old cautious hucksters,
> Taking myself the exact dimensions of Jehovah,
> Lithographing Kronos, Zeus his son, and Hercules his
>   grandson,
> Buying drafts of Osiris, Isis, Belus, Brahma, Buddha
>   (41:1026–1030)

Whitman measures himself for divinity, recognizing the different gods for the work they have done in their various cultural contexts. But at the same time he aspires to invent a deity worthy of a new era of democracy, a deity we need to discover in ourselves and recognize in our fellow travelers.[15]

The National Bard: Loving America

Underlying the different loves of Whitman's Song is a great love for America and its democratic heritage. Here too an allegorical streak can be detected. Whereas traditional Christian allegorists of the Song set out to envision a communal love between God and the Church, Whitman calls for an amorous dialogue between the national bard and the Spirit and Land of America. In the preface to the 1855 edition of *Leaves of Grass*, he defines the national bard as one who must "be commensurate with a people. . . . His spirit responds to his country's spirit. . . . [H]e incarnates its geographies and natural life and rivers and lakes." He goes on to claim that "of all nations the United States with veins full of poetic stuff most need poets and will doubtless have the greatest and use them the greatest." He takes Herder's notion that great poetry (such as the Canticles) "is always the result of a national spirit" a step further and finds its utmost incarnation in the United States and (implicitly) in his own poetry.[16]

In "Song of Myself," more than in any other poem of *Leaves of Grass*, Whitman positions himself as the grand poet-prophet and lover of America and provides detailed catalogues of the variegated folk of America, whose lives he portrays as commensurate with his own. In Section 15, the longest catalogue of all (both ridiculed by early readers and emulated by many admirers, from Allen Ginsberg to Barack

Obama), he offers nearly seventy-five lines of images and sounds of people engaging in various activities. The singing of the pure contralto is the opening note, followed by an unending list of diverse figures, among them the duck-shooter, who "walks by silent and cautious stretches"; the "clean-hair'd Yankee girl who works with her sewing machine"; the "prostitute who drags her shawl"; and the "President holding a cabinet council." The catalogue ends with a climactic declaration: "And these tend inward to me, and I tend outward to them / And such as it is to be of these more or less I am / And of these one and all I weave the song of myself" (15:327–329).

Paradoxically, "Song of Myself" is a song of love that is both self-centered and distinctly communal. If the lover of the Song addresses his beloved with the endearing words, "My sister my lover," Whitman unabashedly seeks the love of all men and women as brothers, as sisters, and as lovers: "And that all the men ever born are also my brothers, and the women my sisters and lovers."

From Whitman's boisterous Song, a poem cherished by many, we turn to Melville's cryptic homage to the Song, barely known outside a limited circle of ardent Melvilleans. However obscure it may be, *Clarel* too is part and parcel of the story of the reception of the Song in American culture, representing a phenomenal experiment with literal and allegorical readings that is far more critical of American dreams than Whitman's "Song of Myself."

Melville's *Clarel*: Poem and Pilgrimage

"Though I wrote the Gospels in this century, I should die in the gutter," wrote Melville to Hawthorne in June 1851 as he was putting the final touches on his "Whale."[17] That Melville could anticipate the failure of his grand all-encompassing Bible did not make the lack of recognition that followed the publication of *Moby-Dick* any easier. Melville kept on writing after this major blow, but he did not venture to fashion a new text of scriptural scope until he set to work on *Clarel*. Published in 1876, *Clarel: A Poem and Pilgrimage in the Holy Land* is a gigantic four-part poem of eighteen thousand dense, constricted, labyrinthine lines that offers an even more obsessive and excessive juggling of biblical texts than *Moby-Dick*. Years after its publication, Melville would describe *Clarel* as a "metrical affair, a pilgrimage or what not, of several thousand lines, eminently adapted for unpopularity."[18] His new Bible was by no means an attempt to make his exegetical imagination more palatable to the reading public.[19]

In *Clarel*, Melville attempts no less than to rewrite the Bible as a whole—there is hardly a scriptural text that is not evoked profusely. But given that he now ventures to write a scriptural poem rather than a scriptural novel, his debt to biblical poetry is significantly greater. The Song of Songs is in many ways the ultimate Poem whose traces Melville seeks in the Holy Land.[20] If *Clarel* is a "Poem and Pilgrimage," as the subtitle indicates, it is because it is a Pilgrimage in search of a grand Poem or a Poem that strives to be a momentous Pilgrimage in its own peculiarly blasphemous way.[21] What makes the Song most suitable for an aesthetic pilgrimage is its insistence on representing love as evasive. The Shulamite and her lover are engaged in an ongoing search, finding and losing each other in rapid transitions. *Clarel*'s loves are of a darker hue and different in character than those of the Song, but they too reveal moments of deep yearning that remain unfulfilled.

Clarel had its beginnings in Melville's journal entries during a three-week voyage to Palestine in 1857. His trip to the Levant was meant to serve as inspiration for a literary comeback, but the notes he wrote at that time reveal nothing but despair and disillusionment. "No country," he declares in his journal, "will more quickly dissipate romantic expectations than Palestine—particularly Jerusalem. To some the disappointment is heart sickening. &c."[22] On his return, he wrote no Holy Land travel narrative that would pave his road back to the limelight. His voyage to the Orient seemed, above all, to confirm his deep suspicion of the standard Holy Land travel narratives of his day.[23]

And yet, in 1866, while working as an inspector for the New York Custom House, Melville started, almost despite himself, to write a long narrative poem about a pilgrimage in the Holy Land. The journey he envisioned was like nothing else in the thriving realm of nineteenth-century American Holy Land travel literature. While mocking the urge of authors of such narratives to find "concrete traces" of biblical texts in Palestine, Melville also ridicules their use of the Holy Land as an exegetical screen against which to reaffirm American exceptionalism. If most American travelers to Palestine were proud to post the American flag on their tents or caravans, Melville's infidel Song offered a dark, cryptic probing of America's landscapes of belief that was not meant to further the Puritan errand.

The protagonist, Clarel, a young Protestant American divinity student whom Melville defines as "pilgrim-infidel" (1.6.19), is prompted by an agonizing theological crisis to travel to Palestine.[24] In Jerusalem, the first station in his pilgrimage, he falls in love with Ruth (modeled both on her biblical namesake and on the Shulamite), a Jewish American woman whose "virgin eyes" make his heart "swell / Like the first tide that ever pressed / Inland, and of a deep did tell" (1.24.70–72). Prevented from seeing Ruth during her mourning for her murdered father, Clarel sets out with a group of pilgrims to tour the Holy Land. In the course of this sojourn, he meets a colorful gallery of pilgrims, messianic madmen, millennialists, ascetics, skeptical scientists, and adventurous travelers of diverse cultural backgrounds and religious creeds. Instead of finding concrete "evidence" of scriptural truths, Clarel discovers that the Bible can be read in perplexingly different ways along the pilgrim routes of Palestine. The desolate Holy Land only complicates his theological doubts and questions.

Throughout *Clarel* Melville evokes the effects, forms, and moods of the Song while projecting it onto the vast canvas of his own poem-pilgrimage in the Holy Land. In so doing he re-creates something of the dreamlike qualities of the biblical poem. In the Song, we move unexpectedly from the lover's garden to the desert, from the hills of Jerusalem to the vineyards of Ein Gedi by the Dead Sea. Being the somnambulist pilgrimage that it is, *Clarel* too shifts between different sites—from Jerusalem down to the Jordan and the Dead Sea and then up to Jerusalem again through the monastery of Mar Saba and Bethlehem. The pilgrims' voyage takes place primarily in the realm of reflections, dreams, and daydreams. Floating voices—whose origins are not easily determined—come and go in fragmentary dialogues.

As is the case with Whitman, it is difficult to assess the degree of Melville's exposure to Herder's writings, but he must have been familiar with secondary sources and well aware of the new continental trends that had been introduced into the exegetical world of the Song. In evoking these new literalist approaches to the Song in *Clarel*, Melville probes their interpretive potentialities but also takes into account the anxieties they generate. A canto titled "The Prodigal" dramatizes the rift.

> "But Palestine,"
> Insisted Clarel, "do you not
> Concede some strangeness to her lot?"
> "*Amigo*, how you persecute!

You all but tempt one to refute
These stale megrims. You of the West,
What devil has your hearts possessed,
You can't enjoy?..."

"Well, me for one, dame Judah here
Don't much depress: she's not austere—
Nature has lodged her in good zone—
The true wine-zone of Noah: the Cape
Yields no such bounty of the grape..."

"Methinks I see
The spies from Eshcol, full of glee
Trip back to camp with clusters swung...

And, tell me, does not Solomon's harp...

confirm the festa? Hear:
'Thy white neck is like ivory;
I feed among thy lilies, dear:
Stay me with flagons, comfort me
With apples; thee would I enclose!
Thy twin breasts are as two young roes.'" (4.26.140–178)

"The Prodigal" provides the most elaborate consideration of the Song in *Clarel*, dealing as it does with an extensive debate between the Lyonese (the so-called "Prodigal" of the canto) and Clarel over the right interpretation of the biblical love poem. Their debate—which takes place at night in a room they happen to share in Bethlehem—opens with the question of how to read the sacred geography of Palestine. Whereas

Clarel traces in Palestine's landscapes strange marks of doom and desolation, the young French salesman from Lyon ventures to read "Dame Judah" as a delightfully voluptuous "wine-zone." Like every respectable exegete, the Lyonese has his proofs. In a typical moment of excessive allusiveness, he offers a series of biblical references, beginning with Noah's drunkenness, moving on to the spies of Eshcol with their great cluster of grapes, and ending with a climactic citation of mismatched versets of some of the most erotic verses of the Song of Songs (4.26.174–178). The scenes that he evokes seem to crop up from the surrounding setting. He can, as it were, "see" the spies tripping back to camp "with clusters hung" on their shoulders and "hear" fragments of the amorous dialogue between the Shulamite and her loved one. Mocking Clarel for being trapped in Western melancholy, the Lyonese suggests that traveling in the East with open ears and eyes may yield unexpected exegetical insights. "Solomon's harp" confirms his pleasurable outlook and serves as a decisive exegetical clue.

The Lyonese is precisely the kind of literalist reader Herder rebukes. He hesitates neither to flaunt the seductive aspects of the Song nor to associate it with the hedonism of wine feasts in the Orient. Teasingly, he calls upon Clarel to admit his fascination with the beauty of Jewish "donnas" and urges him to relinquish his allegorical readings and to "look at straight things more in line" (4.26.200).

Clarel cannot match the imaginative exegetical ingenuity of the Lyonese, but he too has sources:

Clarel protested, yet as one
Part lamed in candor; and took tone
In formal wise: "Nay, pardon me,
But you misdeem it: Solomon's Song
Is allegoric—needs must be." . . .

Why, *Saint* Bernard . . .

The Song's hid import first unrolled—
Confirmed in every after age:
The chapter-headings on the page
Of modern Bibles (in that Song)
Attest his rendering, and prolong:
A mystic burden." (4.26.179–193)

The baffled Clarel evokes Saint Bernard's sermons on
the Song, Christianity's masterpiece of the spiritual
path of love, to prove its "mystic burden." And with
an amusing naïveté, he goes on to trace the confirmation of the allegorical approach in the "chapter-
headings" of "modern Bibles." Most Bibles in
nineteenth-century America were indeed editions of
the King James Version, which included supplemen-
tary guidelines for allegorical reading at the opening
of each chapter of the Song.

In the dialogue between Clarel and the Lyonese,
Melville explores the intricacies of the crisis that arose
in the post-Enlightenment clash between traditional
allegorical readings and newer notions of the plain
sense of the text. Unlike his protagonist, however,
Melville refuses to lose either the pleasures of literal

readings, with their sensual immediacy and oriental flavor, or the complex signification that allegory can offer, especially if one ventures to go beyond traditional exegetical topics. With distinct poetic license, Melville doesn't hesitate to evoke Saint Bernard's sermons and literalist readings of the Song in one canto.

Clarel and Vine: "A Fountain Sealed"

In his 1851 letter to Hawthorne (the same letter in which he foretells the fate of *Moby-Dick*), Melville imagines a blasphemous Paradise into which the two writers will smuggle champagne and where they will cross "their celestial legs in the celestial grass," striking their "glasses and [their] heads together, till both musically ring in concert." Their worldly suffering will then seem the indispensable ingredient that nourished the vine whose grapes were used in the making of the exquisite champagne they'll be drinking.[25] Melville speaks of a heavenly Paradise, but the wine drinking and lounging on the grass endow the scene with the hues of another paradise: the Song's gardens of love, with their intoxicating sensual pleasures.

Something of the tumultuous friendship of these two writers, with its homoerotic overtones, is reenacted in Melville's portrayal of the bond between Clarel and Vine.[26] Vine, the most heretical and reflective traveler in this poem and pilgrimage, arouses much passion in Clarel's heart. In fact, the young divinity student is far more obsessed with his fellow traveler than with Ruth. His admiration for the reserved Vine is so singularly great that at one point he envisions him through the Song's language of love: "Yet Vine could lure / Despite reserve," he muses, "Finding that heart a fountain sealed" (2.17.20–22).

The verse that seeps into Clarel's mind as he watches Vine is: "A garden inclosed is my sister, my spouse; a spring shut up, a fountain sealed" (Song 4:12). The locked garden and the sealed fountain highlight the Shulamite's feminine vitality and cherished virginity. They are, however, set within a sequence in which landscapes and metaphors merge into one another. The beloved is likened to a fountain and a garden— but the garden with its fountains is also the site where the lovers meet or dream of meeting. In the subsequent dream sequence, the dripping myrrh from the beloved's body onto the "handles of the lock" (Song 5:5) intimates that the fountain is not as sealed as it may at first seem.

Vine is set in the position of the Shulamite, sealed and impenetrable yet seductively open—or, rather, semi-open at rare moments. One such moment is evident in the canto "Vine and Clarel," in which the two, in an exceptional scene of dreamy intimacy, recline side by side on the bank of the Jordan River in a "green retreat" of willows and twigs reminiscent of the watery gardens and green bowers of the Song. Here too landscapes and metaphors intersect. Clarel, who first watches the "Venetian slats" created by the play of "light sprays" on the "leafy screen" fall upon Vine's brow and then listens to his ruminations about the waters of the Jordan and the charms of the surrounding sights and sounds, is suddenly drawn to Vine (in his musings) with great intensity:

> So pure, so virginal in shrine
> Of true unworldliness looked Vine.
> Ah, clear sweet ether of the soul
> (Mused Clarel), holding him in view.
> Prior advances unreturned
> Not here he recked of, while he yearned—
> O, now but for communion true
> And close; let go each alien theme;
> Give me thyself! (2.27.62–70)

The young divinity student is magnetized by what he perceives as Vine's virginal purity. He speaks of Vine's soul and unworldliness, but the entire scene by the Jordan River is unmistakably erotic. Confused by this mixture of the ethereal and the bodily, Clarel's exclamation, "Give me thyself!" remains a silent cry.

Like Whitman, Melville juggles literal and allegorical readings of the Song at once, conflating earthly and spiritual loves. Like Whitman, he blasphemously lowers God to the level of the grass and explores the power of homoerotic longings. And yet Melville's Song, unlike Whitman's unbound Song, knows the frustrating limits of freedom; it relentlessly probes and intensifies the fissures between fierce erotic musings and equally fierce inhibitions.

The difference between the respective Songs of Melville and Whitman is most apparent on the national level. Melville cannot but question the optimistic, all-encompassing Whitmanian love for America. Instead of assuming the role of a national bard who spells out his passion for America through detailed catalogues of its folk, Melville composes a poem in which solitary figures yearn for love but are incapable of forming enduring friendships, let alone a community. Clarel's beloved, Ruth, dies, and so do a number of pilgrims along the road; his homoerotic love for Vine is never fulfilled; and God is not quite a lover with whom one can celebrate the democratic spirit but rather an even bleaker "sealed fountain" than Vine: "One tries to comprehend a man, / How think to sound God's deeper heart!" (2.33.110–111).

"I Am Black, but Comely": The Emergence of the African American Song

While Whitman and Melville were carving out their ultimate poems, the Song emerged in a distinctly different form in nineteenth-century African American writings. You will not find verses of the Song in the realm of slave spirituals, where Moses, Joshua, and Jesus prevail, but it does become a notable biblical source in slave narratives and abolitionist rhetoric. Being privileged neither in the foundational moments of American culture nor in earlier exegetical scenes of black culture, the Song had the advantage of marking a new abolitionist spirit.

It comes as no surprise that the most privileged lines of the Song in black culture are those of the Shulamite in her opening declaration: "I am black, but comely O ye daughters of Jerusalem / as the tents of Kedar, the curtains of Solomon / Look not upon me, / because I am black, because the sun hath looked upon me" (Song 1:5–6). The beloved's bold affirmation of her black beauty served as an uplifting source of inspiration for African Americans who sought to dismantle racist presuppositions in the mid nineteenth century. Zilpha Elaw, an African American preacher, speaks in favor of associating "comeliness with blackness" in her 1846 *Memoirs*; Frederick Douglass, the renowned abolitionist, remarks in an 1849 review of *A Tribute for the Negro* that the verse "'I am black but comely' is as true now as it was in the days of Solomon"; and Hannah Craft, in the recently found *The Bondwoman's Narrative* (1850s), uses Song 1:6 as an epigraph for her tale to implicitly comment on the tragedy of a fair-skinned mulatta who tried passing for white.[27]

The African American trend of underscoring the Shulamite's blackness continued in the twentieth century. W. E. B. Du Bois evokes the entire sequence of Song 1:5–6 in *The Souls of Black Folk* (1903) as an epigraph to a chapter titled "Of the Black Belt," in which he depicts the agonies of former slaves in the South in a sharp critique of new forms of racial inequality.[28] Poets and writers of the Harlem Renaissance followed suit and adopted the Shulamite's words in their attempt to fashion a new black aesthetics and a new sense of black heritage. Countee Cullen ends his poem "Black Majesty" (1930) with the lines: "'Lo, I am dark, but comely,' Sheba sings. / 'And we were black,' three shades reply, 'but kings.'"[29] Cullen endorses the Ethiopian tradition according to which the African Queen of Sheba was not merely a visitor to Solomon's court but also the king's beloved. In doing so, he endows African American culture with a glorious founding dynasty that can be traced back to biblical times. Langston Hughes offers a similar view, though adapted for a younger audience, in his children's book, *The First Book of Negroes* (1952): "Sometimes Terry's grandmother tells him true stories about the brown kings and queens in ancient lands. She says the Queen of Sheba, whom King Solomon loved, was an Ethiopian. . . . From the Song of Songs she read 'I am black but comely, O ye daughters of Jerusalem' to show Terry that black people were well known in Biblical times."[30]

The famous slogan of the 1960s—"Black is beautiful"—was, in part, a product of this interpretive scene, though its proponents never evoked Song 1:5 explicitly. The slogan and its cultural frame had an immediate impact on the translation of Song 1:5. Up until the 1970s, the tendency was to follow the King James Version's choice of "but" in English translations of Song 1:5. In Marvin Pope's translation of 1977, by contrast, the verse is translated as "Black am I and beautiful," and in the 1989 New Authorized Version of the Bible it appears as "I am black and beautiful." Biblical translation is forever cultural translation as well. The *ve* of *shehora 'ani ve-nava* may be translated either as "but" or "and," but the changing cultural position of the African American community made the latter option far more appealing.

Toni Morrison: The Flying Solomon

Toni Morrison's oeuvre is undoubtedly the most monumental chapter in the exegetical history of the Song in African American culture. She doesn't merely bolster the Shulamite's affirmation of black beauty in Song 1:5 but draws on the Song of Songs as a whole in probing the untold story of the tormented loves of slaves and former slaves. In two novels—*Song of Solomon* (1977) and *Beloved* (1987)—Morrison carves out grand Songs that are set against the backdrop of two formative periods in the history of African Americans: the era of slavery in the South and the aftermath of the Great Migration to the North. These two novels, among her most acclaimed, were vital to the decision to award Morrison the Nobel Prize in Literature in 1993.

What makes Morrison's readings of the Song all the more riveting is her capacity to continue the project of her African American precursors while addressing questions of gender. Whether or not Morrison was familiar with Phyllis Trible's reading of the Song while writing *Song of Solomon*, the two began to explore the feminist potentiality of the Song at roughly

FIGURE 7. Cover of Toni Morrison's novel *Song of Solomon*, 1977, Penguin Books, first edition.

the same time. Both Morrison and Trible are fascinated by the Shulamite's assertive voice, her daring eroticism, and the unconventional gender configurations in the Song. And yet there are distinct differences between their approaches. Morrison's lovers do not roam about peacefully in an idyllic amorous Paradise but rather wander in the haunted streets and houses of former slaves, where verses such as "I am sick of love" (Song 5:8) and "for love is strong as death" (Song 8:6) acquire uncanny force, highlighting the darker facets of love in the ancient poem.

The title *Song of Solomon* invites us to read Morrison's novel in light of its biblical precursor.[31] What would happen, Morrison ventures to ask, if we were to transfer the Song from biblical times to the world of African American communities in the North between the 1930s and the rise of the civil rights movement? The novel opens in 1931 with the birth of Macon—better known by the nickname Milkman—the first black baby to be born in "No Mercy Hospital," as the African American community calls it. The entrance of the black family to the delivery room takes place right after an insurance agent jumps off the hospital's roof. As a crowd gathers below, a mysterious black woman appears and suddenly "burst[s] into song":

> O Sugarman done fly away
> Sugarman done gone
> Sugarman cut across the sky
> Sugarman gone home . . .[32]

Later we discover that the singing woman is Pilate, Milkman's aunt. From the outset, Pilate is positioned within the realm of songs, but her affiliation with the Shulamite goes beyond her passion for singing. Pilate turns out to be something of an exegetical guide to a new understanding of both the Song and black aesthetics.

Pilate could have easily declared with the Shulamite, "I am black, but comely," even though no one else in her vicinity regards her as such. The end of slavery and the Great Migration to the North by no means led to a miraculous relinquishing of racial prejudices by liberated slaves who were taking their first steps within a highly restricted free world. The craving of many of the black characters in *Song of Solomon* (and there are hardly any white characters) is to be white or whiter. Pilate is the notable exception. From the moment she appears, singing her "Sugarman" song, Pilate never tries to change her appearance or hide her blackness. Macon, her brother, regards her as "a regular source of embarrassment" (20). Not only is she unkempt, refusing to adopt traditional gendered dress (a sailor cap pulled far down over her forehead), but she runs a wine house and "had a daughter but no husband, and that daughter had a daughter but no husband." Macon is furious at his sister for cutting "the last thread of propriety" but cannot stop her. Pilate moves on to construct her own kingdom of female outcasts on the outskirts of town with her daughter Reba and granddaughter Hagar.

Morrison goes beyond the scope of previous African American evocations of the Song, breathing new life into the entire sequence of Song 1:5–6. To better appreciate Morrison's take on these verses, it is worthwhile to dwell on their nuances:

> I am black, but comely, O ye daughters of Jerusalem,
> as the tents of Kedar, as the curtains of Solomon.
> Look not upon me, because I am black,
> because the sun hath looked upon me:
> my mother's children were angry with me;
> they made me the keeper of the vineyards;
> but mine own vineyard have I not kept. (Song 1:5–6)

Whether or not one translates the opening of Song 1:5 as "black but comely" or "black and comely," within the sequence of the Shulamite's declaration either rendition needs to be read as a flagrant rejection of customary views. Against those whose gaze is unfavorable, against those who regard her dark skin as shameful, the beloved rejects normative views and likens her black beauty to the nomadic tents of Kedar (made out of black goat hair) and the glorious pavilions of King Solomon, dyed, in royal fashion, deep black or purple. Hers is a beauty that encompasses all modes of blackness, from rustic to royal. She is as provocative here as she is in announcing, "I am a wall, and my breasts like towers" (Song 8:10). In relishing her dark beauty, the Shulamite celebrates her body and insists on her freedom to experience love in whatever way she deems right. Her black complexion is the outcome of being "looked upon" by the sun while working as a "keeper of the vineyards." But given that the Song is replete with double entendres, the Shulamite may be intimating that despite the reproach of her brothers (her "mother's children"), she wouldn't hesitate to violate traditional norms of female modesty. Brazen as ever, the Shulamite flaunts her tanned skin, her exposure to the warm touch of the sun, and teasingly admits that though a "keeper of the vineyards," she has not kept her "own vineyard." That the vineyards are among the sites where the lovers meet adds an erotic tinge to her words, as do the lavish metaphors that describe the lover's love as "better than wine" (Song 1:2).

If Zilpha Elaw could not have spelled out the Shulamite's uncompromising eroticism in the nineteenth century, Morrison, who wrote against the backdrop of a greater acknowledgment of black aesthetics and a growing corpus of feminist literature and thought in the 1970s, does so in bold strokes. Pilate is a larger-than-life Shulamite who ventures—despite her brother's contempt—to disregard traditional sexual and gender roles. Her making and selling of illegal wine in the secluded "wine house" may be seen as an intriguing variation on the Shulamite's lawless "keeping of the vineyards." And yet Pilate, much like the Shulamite, violates social conventions but follows her own set of codes. No one is allowed to drink on the premises of the wine house, nor does Pilate ever taste the wine she makes.

Pilate's granddaughter doesn't quite follow in her grandmother's footsteps. Hagar is a modern counterpart of her biblical namesake, but she is also a lovesick Shulamite whose love is so deadly that she ventures to take a butcher knife in her hand and roam the streets in search of her lover and cousin, Milkman.[33] Hagar's wandering in quest of her vanished lover calls to mind the Shulamite's dreamlike nocturnal meandering in Song 5. In Morrison's *Song of Solomon*, however, the dark undertones of the Song are intensified. Hagar's lovesickness is more "affliction than affection," and accordingly, the expression that best captures its essence is not "I sleep, but my heart waketh" but rather "her heart beat like a gloved fist against her ribs." Hagar feels an internal blow, as if a fist were crushing her heart. She sets out to seek revenge outdoors or, rather, to search for a weapon that can convey to her lover the misery that has taken hold of her body and soul. And if in the Song incestuous cravings—"O that thou wert as my brother / that sucked the breasts of my mother!" (Song 8:1)—remain on the level of fantasy, in *Song of Solomon* literal incest is at stake, adding a disturbing twist to the maladies of love.

It is left to Milkman to follow (if unwittingly) Pilate's invitation to reconsider blackness. His voyage to the South, to the site of his ancestors' enslavement, allows him to reject his parents' adoration of whiteness. In the arms of Sweet, his southern beloved, he finds a new mode of love, one without the troubling shades of his incestuous bond with Hagar. The lovemaking scene in which Milkman and Sweet bathe each other seems to capture the joyful mutuality of courtship in the Song, as it dramatizes the verse "I am black, but comely." Milkman's body parts are depicted in loving detail, and Sweet's skin, we are told, "squeaked and glistened like onyx" (288).[34]

In the course of his travels in the South, Milkman, as it were, sheds his nickname (given to him in light of his mother's prolonged nursing, yet also associated with the whiteness of milk) and discovers the name of an ancestor he never heard of before: Solomon. "The fathers may soar / And the children may know their names" is the epigraph of *Song of Solomon*. Milkman, at this point, indeed wants to learn about soaring fathers and to "know their names."

Who then is Morrison's Solomon? On first reading the novel's title we assume that *Song of Solomon* refers to King Solomon's Song. But on reaching the concluding episodes it becomes clear that we have expected to find the familiar canonical texts in their recognizable form all too easily. Milkman's voyage through space and time to the South uncovers a legendary ancestral Solomon—a slave who can soar above the agonizing work in the cotton fields and fly back to Africa. Milkman discovers the key to his ancestor's story in a song sung by the children of the town of Shalimar:

Jake the only son of Solomon
Come booba yalle, come booba tambee
Whirled about and touched the sun
Come konka yalle, come konka tambee . . .

Solomon and Ryna Belali Shalut
Yaruba Medina Muhammet too.
Nestor Kalina Saraka cake.
Twenty-one children, the last one Jake!

O Solomon don't leave me here
Cotton balls to choke me
O Solomon don't leave me here
Buckra's arms to yoke me

Solomon done fly, Solomon done gone
Solomon cut across the sky, Solomon gone home.
   (306–307)

This song is none other than the "old blues song Pilate sang all the time," "O Sugarman don't leave me here," Milkman ruminates, except that the children sing, "Solomon don't leave me here" (303). The refrain resembles Pilate's song, but the full song, as it emerges in the South, reveals an entire genealogy whose founding father is the flying Solomon.

Oral culture turns out to be the greatest repository of communal history—thriving as it does on the margins, among women singers and children. Morrison's goal is not to trace the folk "origins" of the Song in a Herderian fashion, but she is attuned to the folkloric quality of the ancient love poem and reformulates it via African American folk songs. In doing so, she confirms W. E. B. Du Bois's view in *The Souls of Black Folk* that the "Negro folk-song—the rhythmic cry of the slave," though initially neglected and despised, "remains the singular spiritual heritage of the nation and the greatest gift of the Negro people."[35] She may also be reinforcing DuBois's choice to accompany the epigraph from Song 1:5–6 in "Of the Black Belt" with three lines of musical notes, intimating that these verses need to be sung.

In incorporating stories about black people who can fly, Morrison oscillates between presenting these tales as an alluring fantasy of escape and taking them seriously as part of an enchanted reality. She relies not only on tales that circulated in her family but also on *Drums and Shadows: Survival Studies Among the Georgia Coastal Negroes* (1940), a compilation of African American folktales translated from Gullah.[36] In some of these tales, a moment before taking off, the slaves chant the magical words Morrison evokes in her "O Solomon" song: "Wa kum kum munin / Kum baba yano / Lai lai tambee / Ashi boong a nomo . . ."[37] In *Song of Solomon*, these African rhythms and chants intermingle freely with English words, forming a vibrant blend of African and American modes of singing.

In Morrison's black Bible, an African slave in the South can assume the position of King Solomon, and his religion may be a cross between Christianity and African traditions. What is more, the flying Solomon marries a woman named Ryna, calling to mind the Spanish word for "queen" (*reina*) and, more specifically, the Queen of Sheba. Morrison seems to follow Hughes and Cullen in construing the encounter between Solomon and the Queen of Sheba in 1 Kings as the inaugural scene of an African dynasty.

Once we reach the South with Milkman, we enter allegorical zones. The Song no longer reverberates solely in the realm of individual loves but becomes relevant to the African American community as a whole. Morrison seems to regard the folk song sung by the children of Shalimar as a basis for a cultural renaissance and a new communal love. Here too, as in Herder's writings and Whitman's "Song of Myself," we discover that the ancient love poem can be used to create modern allegories of communal love. And yet the song of the flying black Solomon and his genealogy is a song of a traumatized community whose capacity for renewal is far from certain. The legendary flying Solomon soars up high but leaves his descendants behind, choking in cotton fields, yoked by their enslavers.

Milkman is moved by the grand familial history he discovers in the South and takes pride in belonging to the "flyin motherfuckin tribe" (332). At the very end of the novel, when he flees from Guitar, his close friend and enemy, he ventures to imitate the flight of his grand ancestor and leaps off Solomon's Leap. Morrison deliberately leaves the ending ambiguous—we do not know whether Milkman manages to fly up or finds his death in the abyss below. Reclaiming his African heritage in the South allows him to "ride" the air, but there is much that hinders his flight—from the ongoing racism of both whites and blacks to the scars of slavery and militant black groups such as Guitar's "Seven Days."

There is, however, one distinctly redeeming moment just before Milkman's cliffhanger leap. Hit by one of Guitar's bullets, Pilate turns to Milkman, saying: "Sing a little something for me" (340). Milkman yields to her last request and sings: "Sugargirl don't leave me here / Cotton balls to choke me / Sugargirl don't leave me here / Buckra's arms to yoke me." After she dies in his arms, Milkman looks at her with love and admiration, realizing that "without ever leaving the ground, she could fly." Morrison reminds us that behind the flying Solomon there is a flying Shulamite whose song too is part and parcel of the heritage Milkman discovers in his quest for lost cultural roots.

Beloved: Owning Love

In *Beloved*, Morrison reinvents the ancient love poem yet again while moving closer to the horrors of slavery. The plot of the novel is based in part on the story of Margaret Garner, a fugitive slave from Kentucky who was tracked in Ohio by a slave hunter in 1856. Resisting her children's return to slavery, Garner killed one of them and would have killed all three had she not been stopped. Morrison sets her novel in 1873, in postbellum rural Ohio, and makes memory the pivotal axis. *Beloved* is a book about the ghostly memories that shake the rafters of every ex-slave's house, even decades after the horrors occurred. The ghost who wreaks havoc in Sethe's house is the unsettling spirit of her murdered daughter, Beloved. Beloved acquires her name in the hasty ceremony of her funeral, when the preacher utters the words "Dearly Beloved . . ." Ten minutes of sex with the engraver, "her knees wide open as any grave," enable Sethe to have "the one word that mattered"—"Beloved"—engraved on her daughter's headstone.[38] But the epigraph of the novel from Romans 9:25 suggests that the name "Beloved" also bears biblical echoes—"I will call them my people, / Which were not my people; / And her beloved, / Which was not beloved."

The Song of Songs does not appear as an epigraph alongside Romans 9:25, but it nonetheless seethes throughout the novel, bursting out toward the end in the lyrical, dreamlike monologues of Sethe and her two daughters, Denver and Beloved—the one living and the other joining from the underworld. Each monologue opens with a proclamation that echoes the Song's recurrent affirmations of the amorous bond: "My beloved is mine and I am his" (Song 2:16), "I am my beloved's and my beloved is mine" (Song 6:3), and "I am my beloved's and his desire is toward me" (Song 7:10). In Morrison's adaptation, "beloved" designates both a "loved one" and a name. Sethe declares, "Beloved, she my daughter. She mine" (200); Denver announces, "Beloved is my sister, I swallowed her blood right along with my mother's milk" (205); Beloved opens two of her sequences with an assertion, "I am Beloved and she is mine" (210, 214). The final note of these lyrical sections is a polyphonic song in which all voices blend together as the three women become inseparable:

Beloved
You are my sister
You are my daughter
You are my face; you are me

I have found you again; you have come back to me

You are my Beloved

You are mine

You are mine

You are mine. (216)

Even in the Song of Songs, the possession of love is not taken for granted. The Shulamite's recurrent statements "I am my beloved's" and "My beloved is mine" are not redundant in their parallelism. Her insistence on uttering both phrases underscores the unquenchable desire for reciprocity, the intense craving of lovers to be enfolded in each other, sealed together forever. But in the context of slavery, in which slaves were owned by their masters and family members were severed from each other, possessing love was a gesture on an entirely different scale. Morrison returns to these verses of the Song to reiterate a compulsive yearning for a sense of belonging: each of the female speakers utters these words and then repeats them in the concluding polyphony of "You are mine."

In *Beloved*, Morrison removes the Song from the context of romantic love, focusing instead on the bond between mother and daughter. Important as Sethe's love for Halle and later Paul D. might be, the craving for belonging erupts within the triangle of Sethe and her two daughters. Morrison is attuned to the special position of the maternal in the ancient love poem, but the "mother's house" in *Beloved*, known as 124, is not a blissful maternal home. Rather, it is a haunted house where "love" is not only "as strong as death" but literally immersed in the realm of the dead. Sethe's love for her daughter is so "thick" that she would rather have her killed than enslaved, and in turn, Beloved comes back from the realm of the dead to haunt her mother as a ghost who cannot be laid to rest. The greatest scars of slavery are evident in an attempted redress that goes awry. To reclaim love in 124 means not only to regain the privilege of owning, but also to be violently possessive and utterly possessed.[39]

The ghostly quality of love is not foreign to the Song. With all its passionate avowals of love, the Song is punctuated by moments when the loved one is shown to be in a state of perpetual flight. Morrison foregrounds these moments of disappearance, though she takes the Song's dialectic of the corporeal and the absent a step further, projecting it onto a world of ghosts. *Beloved*, not unlike *Song of Solomon*, offers a unique blend of biblical texts and African American folklore. Morrison once stated that "her belief in ghosts and spirits was as natural as her belief in germs: to believe was part of her heritage."[40] African and African American folklore abound with tales about spirits who cross a river on their way to and from the underworld, as well as stories about spirits who enter the world of the living to advise or harm their family members.

Beloved appears initially as a semi-benevolent spirit who emerges out of the water as "a fully dressed woman" (50) and joins Sethe's household, filling in the lacuna of the missing daughter while helping her mother retrieve traumatic memories of the past. But gradually she is transformed into an avenging demon, a frenzied "devil child" (261) who drives Sethe insane. Beloved is as overwhelming in her presence as in her absence. Taking the shape of a gigantic pregnant woman, "naked and smiling," with "vines of hair twisted all over her head," the ghostly Beloved cannot be exorcised by Sethe alone. In a strange choir (an echo of the choir of the daughters of Jerusalem in the Song?), thirty neighborhood women assemble outside 124 and struggle to exorcise the dazzling ghost with their singing, "building voice upon voice." There is an unmistakable allegorical dimension in this merging of a haunting individual love with a collective song. Already in the communal song of the flying Solomon in *Song of Solomon* we traced an allegorical streak, but in *Beloved* the attempt to rethink collective love via the Song is far more elaborate.[41]

Baby Suggs's Sermon: Communal Love

The key to understanding Morrison's allegorical reading in *Beloved* lies in the braiding together of the Song of Songs, Romans 9:25, and Hosea 2:16–23 (the prophetic text on which Romans 9:25 is based). Morrison was not the first to combine the Song's beloved with prophetic configurations of the nation as God's beloved. This is, after all, the presupposition of any traditional allegorical reading of the Song. In Morrison's hands, however, this allegorical line acquires a different bent. The amorous bond is not between God and the people; rather, it revolves around the very capacity of a community to love itself, to cherish its heritage despite the humiliation and dehumanization of slavery.

Morrison fleshes out her beloved more extensively than Hosea or Romans but departs from the prophetic figuration and allegorical readings of the Song in refusing to privilege the allegorical-communal sphere. She masterfully combines the literal and the allegorical: Beloved is a Shulamite who is both the particular ghost of the murdered daughter and a collective embodiment of the African American community and, above all, of the many slaves who lost their lives during the Middle Passage. She is a ghost who not only haunts her immediate family but can be bumped into by everyone else.

The intertwining of the literal and the allegorical, of intensely painful personal experiences and communal sorrows, is accentuated in the scene at the Clearing, where Baby Suggs, Sethe's mother-in-law and the "unchurched preacher" of the community, delivers a sermon in a passionate prophetic voice:

> "Here," she said, "in this here place, we flesh; flesh that weeps, laughs; . . . Love it hard. Yonder they do not love your flesh. They despise it. They don't love your eyes; they'd just as soon pick em out. No more do they love the skin on your back. Yonder they flay

it. And O my people they do not love your hands. . . .
Love your hands! Love them. . . . The dark, dark
liver—love it, love it, and the beat and beating heart,
love that too." (88)[42]

This self-reflexive moment captures something of
Morrison's own "unchurched" African American vernacular in *Beloved*. Baby Suggs's sermon is a grand
elaboration of "I am black, but comely" and Romans
9:25 all at once. It provides a sweeping inversion of the
traditional preferencing of the soul over the body and
sets out to undo the loathing of black flesh. Black body
parts are hailed with unbridled enthusiasm, and the
sensual love of black flesh is construed as a prerequisite
for the restoration of true liberty and communal love
for an unloved people.

Beloved, however, does not end with an uplifting
sermon of love. Morrison's Song remains unsettling,
just as the question of the value of probing memories
of the lost loves of slavery remains agonizingly open.
In the fragmentary concluding chapter, we are told
time and again, "This is not a story to pass on" (275).
But paradoxically, this is precisely what Morrison
chooses to do. Beloved's story is too horrifying to bear
but too pivotal to forget. Ultimately, no one can control the spectral daughter. Even if Beloved were cast
back into the waters from whence she emerged, her
epitaph would find a way to return and tell the tale
that should not be told. "Beloved," the final word of
the novel, is set on a line of its own—an ending note

that serves as an opening gesture as well. Much as the Shulamite urges her lover in the final line of the Song to flee—"Make haste, my beloved, and be thou like to a roe or to a young hart upon the mountains of spices" (Song 8:14)—as if embracing his ghostly habits, so too Beloved is chased away only to be conjured back up from the realm of the dead.[43]

Black Lives Matter

Some thirty years after the publication of *Beloved*, the Song still plays a vibrant role in contemporary African American culture. Its most striking emergence has been in the prayers, sermons, and websites of women activists within the Black Lives Matter movement. If in the evocations of the 1960s slogan "Black is beautiful" the Song was merely a subtext, in the commentaries that have emerged from the Black Lives Matter movement the Shulamite's embrace of black beauty is explicitly part of the scene. What is more, the dispute over the appropriate translation of Song 1:5—"but" or "and"— remains an ongoing concern. Thus, in September 2015, Onleilove Alston, the executive director of the Faith in New York organization, delivered a prayer, later posted online, in memory of women who had died in police custody, in which she quoted Song 1:5–6 and declared: "When we think about the Black woman's body we see even within our scripture translations that there has been an attempt to diminish its beauty because most

English translations of Song of Songs 1:5–6 will read I am black BUT Beautiful while in the Hebrew the verse can read I am black AND beautiful."[44] This is not merely a philological comment. Alston calls attention to the political implications of preferring "and" to "but" while positioning the translation that affirms black beauty as the only viable and ethical choice.

Six months later, on March 24, 2016, *Sheloves* magazine published a piece by Micky ScottBey Jones titled "I Am Black and Beautiful" that uses Song 1:5 as a point of departure for an associative flow of ruminations on Black Lives Matter:

> #BlackLivesMatter started as a love letter. After another Black boy laid in the street, a victim of fear, racism and bullets and a jury of American peers said no, that Black boy's life is not beautiful, it does not matter, Alicia wrote a love letter on Facebook. A love letter to remind Black people:
>
> You matter.
>
> You are loved.
>
> You are Black and Beautiful
>
> You are not Black but still somehow, some way beautiful. You are Black *and* you are beautiful. Beautiful lips and beautiful brains. Beautiful thighs and beautiful hearts. Beautiful.
>
> #BlackLivesMatter means Black *and* beautiful and yes it must still be said, because even now, in 2016, we are reminded that some would still choose "but" instead of "and."

Like my sisters and I who are a part of this leader-full movement, we have felt the scorn of those who could not see our beauty. Like our sister in Songs who was put to work because she was a StrongBlack-Woman capable of all the physical, emotional and spiritual work of the world, we are often admired for what we do or what we produce but rarely seen for the totality of who we are.[45]

For ScottBey Jones, the Shulamite is nothing less than a black sister from the past, a black sister whose life (still) matters. Jones's deep affinity with the Shulamite is inspired by Toni Morrison, one of the renowned mentors of the Black Lives Matter movement. Traces of *Song of Solomon* appear in the endorsement of black beauty in the face of those who scorn it, and *Beloved* protrudes between the lines of "You Matter / You are loved / You are Black and Beautiful" as well as in the detailed celebration of the black body as a communal treasure. Micky ScottBey Jones would have probably agreed with Macy Gray's assertion (in a Black Lives Matter post devoted to Morrison) that "Toni Morrison defies the saying 'actions speak louder than words,' for her words do not just speak to the reader, they happen to you."[46] And as Morrison's *Song of Solomon* and *Beloved* "happen" to her readers, they acquire the wondrous capacity to travel beyond their immediate context of origin, molding lives and loves in new, unexpected domains of the American Song.

"Flee My Lover and Be Like a Deer or Like a Gazelle on the Spice Mountains"

The Song ends as it begins—with the Shulamite's voice. If in the opening verse the beloved craves a kiss, in the closing verse she declares: "Flee my lover and be like a deer or like a gazelle on the spice mountains." Here too, we witness a downpour of amorous imperatives—but now instead of asking to be kissed or drawn by her lover, the Shulamite chases him away. Seem puzzling? No less puzzling than love. It is a final virtuoso juggling of the literal and the figurative, or a grand finale of the stream of double entendres that has accompanied us all along. The mountains, we know by now, cannot quite be pinned down: they may be both a concrete landscape and a figurative bodyscape— more specifically (we may assume), a metaphor for the beloved's breasts. In demanding that her lover flee to the mountains of spice, the Shulamite thus sends him off but, at the same time, playfully lures him back to explore her body. And perhaps she urges him to disappear only to keep the exhilarating search going, to continue the rapid dreamlike pace of the amorous race in new perfumed zones where the deer or gazelle may be found, "bounding over the mountains" and "leaping over the hills."

Let us go back for a moment and consider the preceding verses. Chapter 8, the final chapter of the Song, is markedly fragmentary and bewildering. It includes dreamlike floating verses such as "Who is this coming up from the desert / leaning on her lover?" and snatches of the beloved's dialogues with the daughters of Jerusalem and with her brothers. In the midst of it, striking aphorisms about love suddenly emerge, delivered by an unidentified speaker[1]:

> Set me as a seal on your heart,
>> as a seal on your arm.
> For strong as death is love,
>> fierce as Sheol is jealousy.
> Its sparks are fiery sparks,
>> a fearsome flame.
> Many waters cannot
>> put out love
>>> nor rivers sweep it away.
> Should a man give
>> all the wealth of his house for love,
>>> they would surely scorn him. (Song 8:6–7)

Proverbial sayings are not found elsewhere in the Song.[2] Their unexpected appearance here sounds like a last attempt to define love, taking up a different genre that may be more effective in solving its riddles (the word *ahava*, "love," is evoked time and again). These aphorisms underscore the immense power of love—a "fearsome flame" no river can extinguish—but concurrently point to its ominous, accompanying shadows—death, jealousy, and the anxiety of scorn.[3] Yet for all their wisdom in capturing the diverse intensities of love, none of these aphorisms is chosen as the poem's final note.

By the end of the chapter—and of the Song—we return to the dialogue between the two lovers, circling back to the mode of discourse that has prevailed throughout as the most pertinent for expressing love. The Shulamite's final words are in fact a whimsical response to the lover's request to hear her singing. Strictly speaking, the lover asks to hear his beloved's voice (rather than song), but given the social setting implied by the presence of the friends, his request seems to be referring to her singing.

> You who dwell in the garden,
> > friends listen for your voice.
> > > Let me hear it.
> —Flee my lover and be like a deer
> > or like a gazelle
> > > on the spice mountains. (Song 8:13–14)

The Shulamite seems to ignore his wish, but she is attuned to the underlying invitation to celebrate the language of love. Fittingly, the beloved echoes her lover's craving for a song, for a performative moment of amorous discourse, by repeating the most peculiar imperative in the Song, "Be like a deer, or like a gazelle," which first appears in 2:17. She doesn't merely liken the lover to a deer or a gazelle but goes so far as to order him *to be like* them, to perform the simile.[4]

She may be intimating that her lover also needs to adopt his own simile—"Your two breasts like two fawns, twins of a gazelle" (7:4)—and merge, as a fawn or gazelle, with her breasts. Performative speech-acts intermingle with acts of love. The language of love, it seems, can only inflame the lovers' love for each other.

Numerous readers have followed suit and embraced the Song's language of love with great fervor. In considering different moments in the biography of the Song, we've discovered a highly diverse line of aficionados: Jewish and Christian interpreters in late antiquity who were involved in disputes over the right interpretation of the Song, medieval Hebrew poets who introduced the Song into the joyful world of courtly banquets, and kabbalists for whom the Song served as a royal road to the celestial realms of the *sefirot*. We've encountered monastic exegetes who were willing to risk their lives in commenting on or translating the Song. We've followed scholars who set the Song on a pedestal as an oriental poetic gem and others who engaged in fieldwork in an attempt to decipher its folkloric origins. We've noted the ongoing interest of women—from sixteenth-century nuns to twentieth-century feminist critics—in the predominant female voice of the Song. We've followed modern poets and writers who defined their own aesthetics via the Song. We ended with its privileged position in the African American community, where it has been cherished as an uplifting biblical source in a redefinition of black aesthetics and as an antidote against racism. For many readers—be they kabbalists in exile, friars in prison, or African American slaves and former slaves—the Song has offered solace through dark nights. For all readers, the Song has served as a cherished key to the riddles of love.

The Song's charm never seems to diminish. It continues to resonate in contemporary culture in highly diverse modes and realms and to play a pivotal role within different religious spheres around the world. It may be found in Christian liturgy (especially liturgical glorifications of Mary) on websites that give aid in the planning of Christian weddings, and in posts and sermons of activists of the Black Lives Matter movement. It is evoked every Friday in Jewish congregations as they welcome the Sabbath with the famous *piyyut* of Rabbi Shlomo Alkabetz, *Lekha Dodi*, "Hymn to the Sabbath," and is a popular component of contemporary Jewish weddings. It thrives in academia, with new scholarly studies on the Song published yearly. It continues to inspire contemporary writers and artists. It is essential to the recent work of the acclaimed Israeli poet Haviva Pedaya, who evokes Zoharic eros within a modernist framework. It acquires a new look in a 1995 series of paintings by the New York–based Jamaican artist Anna Ruth Henriques.[5] Occasionally, it even crops up in films. At one point in the Coen Brothers's 1990 film *Miller's Crossing*, Tom Reagan (played by Gabriel Byrne) offers a delightful remark: "If I'd known we were gonna cast our feelings into words, I'd've memorized the Song of Solomon."

FIGURE 8. Anna Ruth Henriques, *Song of Songs* chapter 3, 1995. This painting is devoted to the nocturnal, dreamlike scene of Song 3. Henriques' work is indebted to polyglot Caribbean traditions—Jewish and Christian, European, American and African, white and black. The artist's own ancestry directly reflects these interwoven traditions. Her father's family has roots in medieval Spain and was one of the earliest Jewish immigrant families to the New World. Her mother, a convert to Judaism, was more typical of the hybrid nature of Jamaican society—coming from a mix of African, Asian, and other European ancestry. Henriques lives between Jamaica and NYC. Courtesy of the artist.

What will the next chapters in the biography of the Song look like? We can predict that the literal and allegorical interpretive lines will continue to intersect with, or haunt, each other in diverse ways. Above all, we can predict that future chapters in the Song's biography will be as replete with unexpected twists and turns as past chapters. Rabbi Akiva couldn't have anticipated the Song's return to the world of banquets in medieval Jewish culture, Origen couldn't have anticipated Herder's debunking of allegory and the rise of the modern literal Song, Herder couldn't have anticipated the return of allegory through the studies of ancient Near East rituals, and Santa Teresa couldn't have anticipated Phyllis Trible's feminist commentaries or ScottBey Jones's search for a black sister in the Song rather than a monastic sister.

Fascinated by the surprises embedded in the Song's life, S. Y. Agnon, the Nobel Prize laureate of modern Hebrew literature, imagines that the most baffling aspects of the Song's circulation were already evident in Solomon's time. His story on Solomon and his Song titled "And Solomon's Wisdom Excelled" (*Va-terev hokhmat shlomo*, 1950) is a peculiar cross between midrashic commentary and fiction. Following the midrashic format, the story opens with a biblical quotation: "And Solomon's wisdom excelled the wisdom of the children of the East, and all the wisdom of Egypt. For he was wiser than all men. . . . He also uttered three thousand proverbs and his songs were one thousand and five" (1 Kings 5:10–12). Agnon then provides a brief survey of several medieval Jewish commentaries on this verse, each attempting to explain the discrepancy between the claim that Solomon wrote numerous proverbs and songs and the fact that the Bible includes only three of his books: the Song of Songs, Proverbs, and Ecclesiastes. Agnon's primary assumption (in accordance with the commentators he cites) is that the verse from 1 Kings must be taken literally (*mamash*), but he ventures to veer from his precursors to speculate that Solomon's unknown oeuvre was not lost, but rather that the wise king hid the songs intentionally. Anticipating his readers' wonder, Agnon asks: "Yet why would Solomon have wanted to hide them?" In response, he provides a playfully serious tale about the twists and turns in Solomon's life and in the life of his Song:

When Solomon was a young man and the divine inspiration was upon him, he composed the Song of Songs—a song greater than all other songs, the choicest of songs—combining both love and fear of heaven. There was one circle in Jerusalem, however, of good-for-nothing sages who would take the holy words out of context and twist the plain meaning. Of these people Solomon observed: "Little foxes that spoil the vineyards" [Song 2:15]. To which vineyard does he refer? To none other than the vineyards of the Lord of Hosts, of the House of Israel. What did this circle of sages say? "Look at Solomon! The people of Israel are building the Temple and he busies himself writing love songs!" These words reached

Solomon. He placed his left hand beneath his head
[Song 2:6] like a man examining his deeds. . . . He
despaired of mankind and wished to flee. Thus said
Solomon: "Flee my beloved" [Song 8:14].[6]

King Solomon is presented here as an author who
strives in vain to control his audience's modes of reading. Verses from the Song are evoked excessively to depict his frustrating experience. The "good-for-nothing
sages" (*hakhmei shav*) who ignore Solomon's allegorical intentions and scorn the king for writing songs of
earthly desire (*shirey heshek*) are construed as the "little foxes" that raid the vineyards in Song 2:15. Taking
the holy words out of context, these critics fail to see
that when Solomon speaks of vineyards he refers to
"none other than the vineyards of the Lord of Hosts"
(Isaiah 27:2–6).

In a desperate attempt to prevent future distortions
and misreadings, the king seeks a place in which to
hide his perfect songs so as to prevent them from falling into unworthy hands.

Solomon went up to the mountain of myrrh and the
hill of frankincense, as it is written: "Before the day
cools and the shadows flee, I will get me to the
mountain of myrrh and to the hill of frankincense"
[Song 4:6]. How do we know that he wanted to hide
his songs? From the following verse: "You are fair,
my love, there is no flaw in you" [Song 4:7]. What
is it that is fair and without blemish? It is the Song
of Songs.[7]

The literal meaning of his Song, however, continues to haunt him. Wandering in the very landscapes of the ancient love poem—from "the mountain of myrrh" to the "nut garden"—Solomon is reminded time and again of the unabashedly erotic fervor underlying the locations he has evoked. When he finally buries his songs in his vineyard at Ba'al Hammon (Song 8:11), perceiving it to be a safe terrain for their keeping, he discovers that during the feast of love (on the fifteenth of Av) the songs spring up from the ground, enticing the young maidens who dance there in search of love: "The young maidens stood and listened. Their lips dripped like honeycomb as their love was aroused."[8] Solomon doesn't give up. He adjures the maidens not to "stir nor rouse love until it pleases," citing the Shulamite's recurrent cautionary words to the daughters of Jerusalem (Song 2:7; 3:5; 8:4). The maidens follow his request and hide the songs in their hearts, but they too seem to be unable to conceal the ultimate song of love. Verses of the ghostly Song that were supposedly forgotten in their hearts (and then supposedly forgotten altogether) crop up in every line of Agnon's tale, coloring every single episode in Solomon's life.

In Agnon's depiction of Solomon's Song, the ancient poem itself becomes the object of love and is seen as analogous to the Shulamite. Not unlike her, the king's Song is a model of perfection, with "no blemish" (Song 4:7). Agnon seems to create via the Song an allegory about literary passions whose intensity may be as engulfing as any other love. But this allegory has the magical touch of the concrete and the literal insofar as it is inextricably intertwined with earthly loves. It is, after all, Solomon's songs (rather than men) that have the enticing power to awaken the dancing maidens, making their lips drip with honeycomb.

Playfully setting traditional exegesis and modern literalism against each other, Agnon moves beyond traditional exegesis both in his solution to the hermeneutic problem of 1 Kings 5:12 and in the special position allotted to poetry. At the same time, he challenges literalizers of the text for ignoring the ways in which the Song never ceases to generate allegorical readings. Even if we are inclined to read the Song literally, that is not entirely a viable option for a text that is replete with metaphors and sexual double entendres that call for a reading between the vines.

Agnon reminds us in this tale that no one, not even the great Solomon, can attain mastery over the meanings of a circulating text. He also reminds us that the Song arouses incomparable love in the hearts of its listeners and readers. It is not the kind of poem that can remain hidden. The passion with which it was composed is far too contagious and its words of love far too precious.

Overwhelmed by the intensities of love, the Shulamite at times adjures the daughters of Jerusalem not to "stir nor rouse love until it pleases." But she knows only too well the impossibility of the injunction. She knows that what makes love the emotion that looms so large in our lives is the very fact that it is uncontrollable, that it continues to surprise us daily as we wander in the bewildering landscapes of our amorous pursuits.

"Flee my lover and be like a deer or like a gazelle on the spice mountains," says the Shulamite to her lover at the very end of the Song. Her words are also directed to us as readers. She chases us away in this moment of farewell but at the same time lures us back again to continue the race after an unstoppable Song.

INTRODUCTION: "Draw Me After You, Let Us Run"

1. Robert Alter's translation of the Song of Songs, *Strong as Death Is Love: The Song of Songs, Ruth, Esther, Jonah, Daniel* (New York and London: W. W. Norton, 2015). Subsequent biblical citations of the Song in the introduction, the first part of chapter 1, chapter 2, chapter 4, and the epilogue are from this translation. I rely on the translation of the King James Version (KJV) in my readings of Christian allegorists (in the second part of chapter 1 and in chapter 3) in accordance with the English translations of Origen and Saint Bernard. I also use the KJV in chapter 5, given that Whitman, Melville, and Morrison rely on this canonical translation. In other citations from the Hebrew Bible throughout the book, I use Robert Alter's new translation: *The Hebrew Bible: A Translation with Commentary* (New York and London: W. W. Norton, 2018).

2. The sound pattern of the "sh" rustle in the first verses of the Song includes the following words: *shir ha-shirim* (Song of Songs) *asher* (which), **Shelomo** (Solomon), *yishakeni* (let him kiss me), *neshikot* (kisses), *shemen* (oil), and *shimkha* (your name). Note that there is a pun in Song 1:2 that highlights the fluidity of the kisses: "Let him kiss me," *yishakeni*, is phonetically similar to the verb *yashkeni*, "let him make me drink."

3. Franz Rosezweig, *The Star of Redemption*, trans. William W. Hallo (Boston: Beacon Press, 1964 [1921]), 202.

4. For more on Solomon as the composer of the Song, see Steven Weitzman, *Solomon: The Lure of Wisdom* (New Haven, CT, and London: Yale University Press, 2011).

5. On the different approaches to the dating of the Song, see Marvin H. Pope, *Song of Songs*, Anchor Bible (New York: Doubleday, 1977), 22–33.

6. The meaning of the name "Shulamite" has been disputed. The most probable derivation is from *Shalem*, a shortened form of "Jerusalem," though the name is linked through puns with Solomon, *Shelomo*, and "wholeness," *shalem*.

7. For more on the dynamics of parallelism in biblical poetry, see Robert Alter, *The Art of Biblical Poetry* (New York: Basic Books, 1985), ch. 1. See also Alter's extensive discussion of the Song's network of metaphors in ch. 8. For more on the metaphoric web of the Song, see Yair Zakovitch, *The Song of Songs* [in Hebrew], Mikra *le*-Yisrael (Jerusalem and Tel Aviv: Magnes/Am Oved, 1992), and Francis Landy, *Paradoxes of Paradise: Identity and Difference in the Song of Songs* (Sheffield, UK: Almond Press, 1983).

8. For more on the dreamlike scene upon the handles of the lock, see Ilana Pardes, *Countertraditions in the Bible: A Feminist Approach* (Cambridge and London: Harvard University Press, 1992), ch. 7.

9. Robert Alter provides an extensive consideration of the artistic dimension of biblical editing in *The Art of Biblical Narrative* (New York: Basic Books, 1981), ch. 7.

10. See Gershon D. Cohen, "The Song of Songs and the Jewish Religious Mentality," in *Samuel Friedland Lectures, 1960–66* (New York: Jewish Theological Seminary, 1966), 1–21.

11. Chapter 4 provides an extensive consideration of the cultic approach.

CHAPTER 1: The Rise of Allegory: From Rabbi Akiva to Origen

1. Jacob Neusner, trans., *Song of Songs Rabbah: An Analytical Translation*, Brown Judaic Studies (Atlanta: Scholars Press, 1989), 2:48.

2. Origen, *The Song of Songs, Commentary and Homilies*, trans. R. P. Lawson (Westminster, MD: Newman Press, 1957), 272–273. All future references are to this edition and will appear in parentheses in the text.

3. On the history of allegory, see Jon Whitman, *Allegory: The Dynamics of an Ancient and Medieval Technique* (Cambridge: Harvard University Press, 1987); Rita Copeland and Peter T. Struck, eds., *The Cambridge Companion to Allegory* (Cambridge and New York: Cambridge University Press, 2010); and Stephen Greenblatt, ed., *Allegory and Representation* (Baltimore and London: Johns Hopkins University Press, 1981).

4. Quoted in Jon Whitman, "A Retrospective Forward: Interpretation, Allegory and Historical Change," in *Interpretation and Allegory: Antiquity to the Modern Period* (Leiden and Boston: Brill, 2000), 3.

5. For an extensive consideration of Romantic perspectives on allegory, see Teresa M. Kelley, "Romanticism's Errant Allegory," in Copeland and Struck, *Cambridge Companion to Allegory*, 211–228.

6. Walter Benjamin, *The Origins of German Tragic Drama*, trans. John Osborne (London: NLB, 1977). For more on Benjamin's perception of allegory, see Howard Caygill's "Walter Benjamin's Concept of Allegory," in Copeland and Struck, *Cambridge Companion to Allegory*, 241–253.

7. *Rabba* means "great," attesting to the sizable volume of *Song of Songs Rabba*. The smaller corpus of midrashim on the Song is known as *Song of Songs Zuta* (*Agadat Shir Ha-Shirim*).

8. *Song of Songs Rabba* draws on Tannaitic literature, the Jerusalem Talmud, *Genesis Rabba*, and *Leviticus Rabba*, as well as *Pesikta de-Rav Kahana*.

9. On the prophetic marital metaphor, see Moshe Halbertal and Avishai Margalit, *Idolatry* (Cambridge: Harvard University Press, 1992), ch. 1.

10. For more on the double personification of God and the nation in Exodus, see Ilana Pardes, *The Biography of Ancient Israel: National Narratives in the Bible* (Berkeley: University of California Press, 2000).

11. Neusner, *Song of Songs Rabba*, 1:56.

12. On the midrashic use of the Song as key to Exodus, see Daniel Boyarin, *Intertextuality and the Reading of Midrash* (Bloomington and Indianapolis: Indiana University Press, 1990), 105–116.

13. My translation. See also Nedarim 50a.

14. Boyarin's translation; quoted in Boyarin, *Intertextuality*, 114. Reprinted with permission of Indiana University Press.

15. The mixture of sights and sounds in Song 2:14 is especially exquisite given the chiastic structure of the two parallelisms. The lover could have said "let me hear your voice, / for your voice is sweet" and "show me how you look, / for your look is desirable," but instead he oscillates between sights and sounds in both parallelisms, creating a delightful mélange of sensual cravings.

16. Boyarin's translation; quoted in *Intertextuality*, 111.

17. See James Kugel, "Two Introductions to Midrash," in *Midrash and Literature*, ed. Geoffrey Hartman and Sanford Budick (New Haven, CT: Yale University Press, 1986), 95.

18. Boyarin's translation; quoted in *Intertextuality*, 113.

19. "Show me thy visage" includes two words whose root is *r'a h*—*har'ini* ("show") and *mar'ayikh* ("visage"). Given that the verb *r'a h* is also used when the people are summoned to witness God's salvation—to "see *(re'u)* the salvation of the Lord"—Rabbi Eliezer regards it as proof of an inherent connection between the two episodes. What is more, he detects a link between the beauty of the Song's beloved (*mar'ekh naveh*) and the beauty of God as it is hailed in the Song of the Sea: "This is my God and I will [beautify] Him (*anvehu*)" (Exodus 15:2). To be more precise, *anvehu* literally means "and I will extol Him," but in light of the phonetic similarity between *nave* and *anvehu*, the two terms are perceived as linked.

20. On the perception of poetry in *Song of Songs Rabba*, see Tamar Kadari, "Song and Meaning: A New Look on Rabbinic Exegesis of the Song of Songs" [in Hebrew], *Jerusalem Studies in Hebrew Literature* 28 (2016): 27–54.

21. For more on the definition of mysticism, see Gershom Scholem, *Major Trends in Jewish Mysticism* (New York: Schocken Books, 1961).

22. For more on the interrelations of the Song and Ezekiel's chariot in early Jewish mysticism, see Yosef Dan, *The Ancient Jewish Mysticism* (Tel Aviv: MOD Books, 1990).

23. Boyarin's translation; quoted in *Intertextuality*, 109–110.

24. For an extended comparison between Rabbi Akiva and Ben Azzai, see Yehuda Liebes, *Elisha's Sin: Four Who Entered the Orchard and Talmudic Mysticism* [in Hebrew] (Jerusalem: Academon, 1990). For a broader consideration of the rabbis' sexual practices, see David Biale, *Eros and the Jews: From Biblical Israel to Contemporary America* (New York: Basic Books, 1992), ch. 2.

25. Neusner's translation with minor variations, 1:87. An earlier version of this renowned tale appears in the Talmud (*Hagiga* 14b). Its reappearance in *Song of Songs Rabba* is accompanied by greater emphasis on the relevance of the Song to this exegetical orchard. Note that whereas in the Talmud Ben Azzai dies, in *Song of Songs Rabba* he only loses his mind (that is, Ben Azzai and Ben Zoma switch roles).

26. The term *pardes* appears in Song 4:13 and forms part of the metaphoric nexus of the beloved as "locked garden."

27. On *Shi'ur Koma* and Merkava mysticism, see Gershom Scholem's *Jewish Gnosticism, Merkabah Mysticism, and Talmudic Tradition* (New York: Jewish Theological Seminary of America, 1960); Scholem, *On the Kabbalah and Its Symbolism* (New York: Schocken Books, 1996), 14–21. For a current reassessment of the date of *Shi'ur Koma*, see Peter Schafer, *The Origins of Jewish Mysticism* (Tübingen: Mohr Siebeck, 2009), 306–314.

28. Saul Lieberman, "Mishnat Shir Ha-Shirim," in Scholem, *Jewish Gnosticism*, 118–126.

29. On the dialogue between Jewish and Christian neighboring communities in late antiquity, see Galit Hasan-Rokem, *Tales of the Neighborhood: Jewish Narrative Dialogues in Late Antiquity* (Berkeley: University of California Press, 2003).

30. For more on Origen's biography, see Rowan A. Greer's introduction to his *Origen: An Exhortation to Martyrdom, Prayer and Selected Works*, Classics of Western Spirituality (Mahwah, NJ: Paulist Press, 1979).

31. See Reuven Kimelman, "Rabbi Yokhanan and Origen on the Song of Songs: A Third-Century Jewish-Christian Disputation," *Harvard Theological Review* 73, nos. 3/4 (1980): 567–595.

32. It is noteworthy that, although Origen was the first Christian exegete to provide a substantive commentary on the Song, he had precursors. Early fragments of allegorical readings of the Song may also be detected in the New Testament; see Peter Tomson, "The Song of Songs in the Teachings of Jesus and the Development of the Exposition on the Song," *New Testament Studies* 61, no. 4 (2015): 429–444. The apocryphal *First Esdras* is another case in point.

33. Quoted in Pope, *Song of Songs*, 114.

34. Origen, *The Song of Songs, Commentary and Homilies*, trans. R. P. Lawson (Westminster, MD: Newman Press, 1957), 23. All future references are to this edition and will appear in parentheses in the text.

35. Scholem discusses Origen's comment on Jewish practices in *Jewish Gnosticism*, 38–40.

36. See Lawson's introduction to Origen's commentary on the *Song of Songs*.

37. On Origen's sense of the Song's perfection, see J. Christopher King, *Origen on the Song of Songs: The Bridegroom's Perfect Marriage-Song* (Oxford and New York: Oxford University Press, 2005), esp. 25–30.

38. Origen adheres to two major interpretive modes, but it is noteworthy that by the fifth century Christianity had developed a fourfold hermeneutic framework analogous to the Jewish *pardes*. Thus John Cassian speaks of four ways of interpreting "Jerusalem": from a historical perspective as the city of the Jews, from an allegorical perspective as the Church of Christ, from an anagogical perspective as the celestial city of God, and from a tropological perspective as an emblem of the soul. See Ann Matter, *The Voice of My Beloved: The Song of Songs in Western Medieval Christianity* (Philadelphia: University of Pennsylvania Press, 1990), 54.

39. Pope, *Song of Songs*, 115.

40. Quoted in Greer's introduction to *Origen: An Exhortation*, 3.

41. For more on Origen's notion of sin and the body, see Paula Fredriksen, *Sin: The Early History of an Idea* (Princeton, NJ: Princeton University Press, 2012), 93–112. On sexuality in early Christianity, see Elaine Pagels, *Adam, Eve, and the Serpent* (New York: Random House, 1988).

42. See David Dawson, *Christian Figural Reading and the Fashioning of Identity* (Berkeley, CA: Berkeley University Press, 2001); and Daniel Boyarin, "Origen as Theorist of Allegory: Alexandrian Contexts," in Copeland and Struck, *Cambridge Companion to Allegory*, 39–56.

43. Neusner's translation, 1:61.

44. On the polemical angle of the Jewish–Christian dialogue on the Song in late antiquity, see Ephraim E. Urbach, "The Homiletical Interpretations of the Sages and the Expositions of Origen on Canticales, and the Jewish-Christian Disputation," *Scripta Hierosolymitana* 22 (1971): 257.

45. For an extensive consideration of the implicit exchanges between Rabbi Yohanan and Origen, see Kimelman, "Rabbi Yokhanan and Origen."

CHAPTER 2. Poets and Kabbalists: From Medieval Hebrew Poetry to the Zohar

1. The notable medieval advocate of the literal sense within the Ashkenazi world was Rashi, Rabbi Shlomo Yitzchaki (1040–1105), a French medieval exegete.

2. The growing acknowledgment of the literal sense in medieval Jewish exegesis is in part indebted to Islamic hermeneutic trends and the cherishing of the *zahir* (literal sense) in the context of Quranic exegesis. See Mordechai Z. Cohen, "Emergence of the Rule of *peshat* in Medieval Jewish Bible Exegesis," in *Interpreting Scriptures in Judaism, Christianity and Islam: Overlapping Inquiries*, ed. Mordechai Z. Cohen and Adele Berlin (Cambridge: Cambridge University Press, 2016), 204–224.

3. *Abraham Ibn Ezra's Commentary on the Canticles*, ed. and trans. H. J. Mathews (London: Trübner and Co, 1874), xi.

For more on Ibn Ezra's biblical exegesis, see Uriel Simon, *The Ears Discern Words: Studies in Ibn Ezra's Exegetical Methodology* [in Hebrew] (Ramat Gan, Israel: Bar-Ilan University Press, 2013).

4. *Abraham Ibn Ezra's Commentary*, 10.

5. *Abraham Ibn Ezra's Commentary*, 13.

6. For an introduction to medieval Hebrew poetry in Muslim Spain, see Peter Cole, *The Dream of the Poem: Hebrew Poetry from Muslim and Christian Spain, 950–1492* (Princeton, NJ, and Oxford: Princeton University Press, 2007), 1–20.

7. Note that love poems are called *ghazal* in Arabic precisely because of the centrality of the figure of the *ghazāl* in this genre. See Raymond P. Scheindlin, *Wine, Women, and Death: Medieval Hebrew Poems on the Good Life* (New York: Jewish Publication Society, 1986), 129.

8. See Scheindlin, *Wine, Women, and Death*, 77–89; and Shulamit Elizur, *Hebrew Poetry in Spain in the Middle Ages* [in Hebrew] (Tel Aviv: Open University of Israel, 2004), vol 2.

9. Scheindlin, *Wine, Women, and Death*, 82–83. For more on questions of gender in medieval Hebrew poetry, see Tova Rosen's *Unveiling Eve: Reading Gender in Medieval Hebrew Literature* (Philadelphia: University of Pennsylvania Press, 2003).

10. That there is another common term for the beloved in Arabic poetry, *zabi*—the Arabic cognate of the Hebrew *tzvi*— reinforced the notion that such hybridity was called for.

11. Peter Cole, *Dream of the Poem*, 45. In Hebrew the moon is depicted as the letter *yod* (a letter whose shape resembles a crescent and begins the word for "wine," *yayin*). In Cole's translation, the D stands for "Drink" and the shape of the half-moon.

12. For more on the wine culture of al-Andalus, see Scheindlin, *Wine, Women, and Death*, 19–33.

13. See Peter Cole, *Selected Poems of Shmuel HaNagid* (Princeton, NJ: Princeton University Press, 1996), 168.

14. Cole, *Dream of the Poem*, 45.

15. The homoerotic dimension of medieval Hebrew poetry has been a topic of scholarly dispute. Homosexuality is forbidden by Jewish law, but whether or not it was more acceptable within the court culture of the Middle Ages remains unclear. The homoerotic poems of HaNagid do not necessarily reflect his personal experiences, but they do express a distinct cultural openness and rejection of homophobia. See Norman Roth, "'Deal gently with the young man': Love of Boys in Medieval Hebrew Poetry of Spain," *Speculum* 57, no. 1 (1982): 20–51; Matti Huss, "*Machberet sheliach ha-tsibbur*: The Question of Sources and Relation to the Homoerotic Hebrew Literature of the Middle Ages" [in Hebrew], *Tarbiz* 64, nos. 1–2 (2002): 197–244.

16. *Divan Shmuel HaNagid*, 221, quoted in Roth, "'Deal gently,'" 35. Note that in addition to HaNagid's poetic comment, his son, Jehoseph, who edited his father's poetic work, explicitly noted in the preface of one of the volumes that HaNagid's love poems should be read allegorically. See Matti Huss, "Secular Poetry or Religious Allegory: The Love Poems of Shmuel HaNagid" [in Hebrew], *Jerusalem Studies in Hebrew Literature* 15 (1994): 35–73.

17. Cole, *Dream of the Poem*, 145.

18. Cole, *Dream of the Poem*, 146.

19. See Scheindlin, *Wine, Women, and Death*, 127.

20. An extended account of the reception of the Song in the early *piyyut* is beyond the scope of this book. For more on this exegetical scene, see Laura S. Lieber, *A Vocabulary of Desire: The Song of Songs in the Early Synagogue* (Leiden and Boston: Brill, 2014).

21. It is unclear whether in late antiquity there was already a custom of reciting the entire text of the Song during Passover. The first known reference to its recitation during Passover is found in *Masekhet Soferim*, one of the Minor Tractates. See Michael Fishbane, *Song of Songs: The JPS Commentary* (Philadelphia: Jewish Publication Society, 2015), xlviii–xlix.

22. In addition to the Song's dove, one can find traces of another biblical dove in this poem: that of Psalm 56:1.

23. Cole, *Dream of the Poem*, 157.

24. See the discussion on *Song of Songs Rabba* in the previous chapter.

25. Cole, *Dream of the Poem*, 91.

26. The liturgical love poem thus transforms into a poem of complaint with a distinctly personal tone (poetry of complaint, *shirey telunah*, another well-known genre of medieval Hebrew poetry, is one of Ibn Gabirol's specialties).

27. Raymond P. Scheindlin's translation in *The Gazelle: Medieval Hebrew Poems on God, Israel, and the Soul* (New York and Oxford: Oxford University Press, 1991), 91. See Scheindlin's reading of the poem in 93–95.

28. Ibn Gabirol's major Neoplatonic opus, *Fountain of Life*, became an important work in the history of Scholastic philosophy (via the Latin translation of the original Arabic). Throughout the Middle Ages and into the nineteenth century, its author was thought to be a Muslim or Christian by the name of Avicebron, Avicembron, or Avicebrol.

29. Translated by Scheindlin, *Gazelle*, 43. For more on the role of the soul in medieval Hebrew poetry, see Scheindlin, *Gazelle*, 137–229; Rosen, *Unveiling Eve*, ch. 4; Adena Tenenbaum, *The Contemplative Soul: Hebrew Poetry and Philosophical Theory in Medieval Spain* (Leiden and Boston: Brill, 2002). For more on the role of the Song in this connection, see Fishbane, *Song of Songs*, 273–275.

30. Some of the liturgical poems of Yehuda HaLevi and Ibn Gabirol were set to music. HaLevi's "A Dove at a Distance" (*Yonat Rechokim*) as well as Ibn Gabirol's "Open the Gate," "The Gate Long Shut" (*Sha'ar Asher Nisgar*), and the popular "Shalom to You, My Beloved" (*Shalom Lekha Dodi*) have over the years circulated in diverse Jewish communities and yielded different musical adaptations. The website of *Hazmanah le-piyyut* offers samples of diverse arrangements.

31. Scholem was not the first to suspect that Moshe de León was involved in writing the Zohar, but he was the first to substantiate the claim.

32. For background on the Zohar and an overview of the different generations of Kabbalah scholars and their respective views, see Arthur Green's introduction to the Pritzker edition of the Zohar: Daniel C. Matt, ed., *The Zohar* (Stanford, CA: Stanford University Press, 2004) 1:31–81; and Haviva Pedaya's "Afterword" to the Hebrew translation of Scholem's *Major Trends* (Tel Aviv: Yediot Ahronot, 2016), 405–415.

33. The most resonant references are to Ibn Gabirol's *Kingdom's Crown* (*Keter Malkhut*).

34. Terumah 2:144a, in Matt, *Zohar*, 5:314. This is only a fragment of an extensive midrashic elaboration on the superlative title of the Song in Zohar Terumah. Another Zoharic corpus that is relevant in this connection is Zohar Hadash; see Joel Hecker's translation and commentary, "Zohar on the Song of Songs," in Matt, *Zohar*, vol. 11.

35. For more on the Shekhinah, see Scholem, *Major Trends in Jewish Mysticism*; Ephraim E. Urbach, *The Sages: Their Concepts and Beliefs* (Jerusalem: Magnes Press, 1975), 37–65; and Moshe Idel, *Kabbalah and Eros* (New Haven, CT, and London: Yale University Press, 2005).

36. Terumah 2:143a, in Matt, *Zohar*, 5:309.

37. See Matt's notes on this commentary.

38. See Shifra Asulin, *The Mystical Exegesis of the Song of Songs in the Zohar* [in Hebrew] (Ph.D. diss., Hebrew University, 2006), 36–43.

39. Idel, *Kabbalah and Eros*, 142–143.

40. Many have written on the parable of the maiden. To mention but a few influential readings, see Gershom Scholem, "The Meaning of Torah in Jewish Mysticism," in *On the Kabbalah*, 55–64; Yehuda Liebes, "Zohar and Eros" [in Hebrew], *Alpayim* 9 (1994): 67–119.

41. Matt, *Zohar*, 5:33–35.

42. This is also a dramatization of the Zoharic *pardes*, an acronym of the four modes of exegesis: *P* for *peshat*, *D* for *drash* (midrashic), *R* for *remez* (philosophical-allegorical), and *S* for *sod* (mystical). For more on the Zoharic exegetical orchard, see Scholem, *On the Kabbalah*, 56–57.

43. Scholem, *Major Trends in Jewish Mysticism*, 27.

44. The authors of the Zohar may have also been influenced by the elegiac mixtures of the Song and Lamentations in early *piyyutim* for Tish'a beAv. Eleazar Kallir's "Woe how the Rose of Sharon sits alone" is but one memorable example.

45. Zohar 3:191a, quoted in Melila Helner-Eshed, *A River Flows from Eden: The Language of Mystical Experience in the Zohar* (Stanford, CA: Stanford University Press, 2009), 224–225.

46. The translation of the King James Version is more appropriate for this Zoharic midrash.

47. Helner-Eshed, *River Flows from Eden*, 204–251.

48. See Helner-Eshed's discussion in *River Flows from Eden*, 224–225.

49. See Arthur Green, "Shekhinah, The Virgin Mary, and the Song of Songs," *AJS Review* 26, no. 1 (2002): 1–44. Green's article generated a heated debate among scholars of Kabbalah. Yehuda Liebes refutes the possibility that Marian worship could have had any impact on configurations of the Shekhinah, one of his major points being the pronounced difference between the virginity of Mary and the overt sexuality of the Shekhinah. See Liebes, "Is the Shekhinah a Virgin?: A Response to Arthur Green" [in Hebrew], *Peamim* 101–102 (2005): 303–313. To be sure, there are important distinctions between the Shekhinah and Mary, but influence, especially in polemical contexts, cannot but be partial.

50. For an extensive comparison of the Shekhinah and Mary, see Peter Schaefer's *Mirror of Her Beauty: Feminine Images of God from the Bible to Early Kabbalah* (Princeton, NJ, and Oxford: Princeton University Press, 2002).

51. Avi Elqayam traces a whole genealogy of roses leading to the Zoharic rose; see his "As a Rose Among the Thorns: The Secret of the Rose as the Image of All Images" [in Hebrew], in *Kabbalah, Mysticism, and Poetry: The Journey to the End of Vision*, ed. Avi Elqayam and Shlomy Mualem (Jerusalem: Magnes Press, 2015), 121–241. He begins with the roses of medieval Hebrew poetry and ends with the Marian rose and the roses of the chivalric sphere, above all *Le Roman de la Rose* (*The Romance of the Rose*).

52. Zohar 1:1a, in Matt, *Zohar*, 1:1.

53. See Matt's notes in *Zohar*, 2–3.

54. Medieval Hebrew poetry was not welcomed by all in Safed. The spiritual leaders of Safed differed in their approach to it: whereas Moses Cordovero (1522–1570) was an aficionado of medieval poetry and endorsed its renewal, Isaac Luria (HaAri) was critical of these works' philosophical Neoplatonic dimension. See Avi Elqayam, "Azamer bi-shvachin: On HaAri's Ars Poetics" [in Hebrew], in *The Piyyut as a Cultural Prism: New Approaches*, ed. Haviva Pedaya (Jerusalem: Van Leer & Hakibbutz Hameuchad, 2012), 68–150.

55. For more on the liturgical poetry of Najara, see Haviva Pedaya's "The Text and Its Performance in the Poetry of Rabbi Israel Najara" [in Hebrew], in Pedaya, *Piyyut as a Cultural Prism*, 29–67.

56. Peter Cole, *The Poetry of Kabbalah: Mystical Verse from the Jewish Tradition* (New Haven, CT: Yale University Press, 2012), 137–138.

57. For an extended analysis of *Lekha Dodi*, see Cole, *Poetry of Kabbalah*, 129–132, 352–360; Reuven Kimelman, *The Mystical Meaning of Lekhah Dodi and Kabbalat Shabbat* [in Hebrew] (Jerusalem: Magnes Press, 2002).

58. See Cole, *Poetry of Kabbalah*, 133–135.

CHAPTER 3. Monastic Loves:
From Saint Bernard to Santa Teresa

1. Interestingly enough, there are many references to the Song in *The Name of the Rose*—primarily in discussions regarding the interrelations of human and divine love. Even the title evokes the metaphoric nexus of the Song's rose and its resonance in Christian exegesis. One of Eco's sources for the title (as he indicates in his *Postscript to the Name of the Rose*) is a poem by Sor Juana Ines de La Cruz, the seventeenth-century Mexican nun and mystic, in which the beauty of the Song's "rose of the valleys" is drawn in gloomier shades.

2. For more on Bernard's life, see the introduction in *Bernard of Clairvaux: Selected Works*, ed. Jean Leclercq (New York: Paulist Press, 1987), 13–57.

3. For an extended discussion of the Latin commentaries on the Song and a detailed consideration of Bernard in this connection, see Matter, *Voice of My Beloved.*

4. For more on the interrelations of Bernard's concept of love and courtly love literature, see Jean Leclercq, *Monks and Love in Twelfth-Century France* (Oxford: Oxford University Press, 1987), 86–108.

5. The term "sermons" is not the only title used in earlier accounts of Bernard's commentary, which suggests that this homiletical corpus may be more literary than oral. See Matter, *Voice of My Beloved,* 123–125.

6. Bernard of Clairvaux, Sermon 1, trans. Ann Matter, in her *Voice of My Beloved,* 125.

7. Jean Leclercq, *The Love of Learning and the Desire for God: A Study of Monastic Culture* (New York: Fordham University Press, 1982), 4.

8. Bernard of Clairvaux, Sermon 1, in *Bernard of Clairvaux: Selected Works,* trans. G. R. Evans (New York: Paulist Press, 1987), 212.

9. Matter, *Voice of My Beloved,* 138.

10. Bernard of Clairvaux, *On the Song of Songs I,* trans. Kilian Walsh (Kalamazoo, MI: Cistercian Publications, 1979), 20.

11. On the feminization of the soul in Bernard's exegesis, see Ann Astell, *The Song of Songs in the Middle Ages* (Ithaca, NY, and London: Cornell University Press, 1990). For a consideration of the homoerotic aspect in Bernard's sermons, see Bruce Holsinger, "The Color of Salvation," in *The Tongue of the Fathers: Gender and Ideology in Twelfth-Century Latin,* ed. David Townsend and Andrew Taylor (Philadelphia: University of Pennsylvania Press, 1998), 164–165.

12. Bernard of Clairvaux, *On the Song of Song IV,* trans. Irene Edmonds (Kalamazoo, MI: Cistercian Publications, 1980), 137–138.

13. On Bernard and the question of affect, see Julia Kristeva, *Tales of Love,* trans. Leon S. Roudiez (New York: Columbia University Press, 1987), 151–169.

14. Bernard, *On the Song of Song IV*, trans. Irene Edmonds, 141.

15. For more on the vernacular Bible, see Jonathan Sheehan, *The Enlightenment Bible: Translation, Scholarship, Culture* (Princeton, NJ: Princeton University Press, 2005), 1–25.

16. See the introduction to Teresa's *Meditations* in *The Collected Works of St. Teresa of Avila*, trans. Kieran Kavanaugh and Otilio Rodriguez (Washington, DC: Institute of Carmelite Studies, 1980), 2:208.

17. The majority of Spain's Jews converted to Christianity during this period—the bulk of them as a result of the pogroms of 1391 and the remainder later in the fifteenth century—to avoid the expulsion of 1492.

18. Catherine Swielicki's *Spanish Christian Cabala: The Works of Luis de León, Santa Teresa de Jesus, and San Juan de la Cruz* (Columbia: University of Missouri Press, 1986) offers the most extensive study in this connection. Collin Thompson endorses a more skeptical view regarding substantive kabbalistic influence in the case of Fray Luis, but his observations may also be relevant to Teresa and John of the Cross—see Colin P. Thompson, *The Strife of Tongues: Fray Luis de Leon and the Golden Age of Spain* (Cambridge: Cambridge University Press, 1988). That cross-cultural currents between the Jewish and Christian worlds were acquiring greater force during this period is evident in the emergence of Christian Kabbalah in Spain. Our three Spanish mystics are not Christian kabbalists but may have been partially influenced by such trends.

19. For more on the role of Mary as the Song's Bride in Christian exegesis, see Astell, *Song of Songs*, ch. 2.

20. *Meditations* 1:1–2, in *Collected Works of St .Teresa of Avila*, 2:216.

21. See Alison Weber, *Teresa of Avila and the Rhetoric of Femininity* (Princeton, NJ: Princeton University Press, 1990), 104–106.

22. *Meditations* 6:7, in *Collected Works of St .Teresa of Avila*, 2:253.

23. Note that while Teresa's work as an exegete was curtailed, some of the books in which she records personal spiritual

experiences—primarily *The Interior Castle* (*El castillo interior*) and *The Way of Perfection* (*El camino de perfección*)—were widely circulated without inquisitorial restrictions.

24. Teresa refers to her nuns as "daughters," *hijas*, in other writings as well, but in the context of her meditations on the Song this term is endowed with a special significance, calling to mind the "daughters of Jerusalem."

25. *Meditations* 2:5, in *Collected Works of St. Teresa of Avila*, 2:224.

26. *Meditations* 1:10–12, in *Collected Works of St. Teresa of Avila*, 2:220–222.

27. On spiritual renditions of the senses, see Aviad Kleinberg, *The Sensual God: How the Senses Make the Almighty Senseless* (New York: Columbia University Press, 2015).

28. There are no written vowels in this Hebrew term, which is why such fluidity is possible. But given the context, "love" is the more appropriate translation.

29. On Christ's nurturing breasts and sexual reversal in medieval culture, see Caroline Walker Bynum's *Holy Feast, Holy Fast: The Religious Significance of Food to Medieval Women* (Berkeley: University of California Press, 1987), esp. 282–288.

30. *Meditations* 4:4, in *Collected Works of St. Teresa of Avila*, 2:244.

31. Milk blends well with wine in the Song—"I have come to my garden, my sister, bride . . . I have eaten my honeycomb with my honey / I have drunk my wine with my milk" (5:1)—endowing nurturance with a sense of intoxication.

32. For more on Teresa's sense of divine intoxication, see Carole Slade, *St. Teresa of Avila: Author of a Heroic Life* (Berkeley: University of California Press, 1995).

33. *Meditations* 6:5, in *Collected Works of St. Teresa of Avila*, 2:252.

34. See in particular the commentary on "Sustain me with flowers and surround me with apples, for I am dying of love" (a somewhat distorted translation of Song 2:5 that bears echoes of Song 8:6) in *Meditations* 7.

35. *Meditations* 1:6, in *Collected Works of St. Teresa of Avila*, 2:218.

36. *The Life of Saint Teresa of Avila by Herself*, trans. J. M. Cohen (New York: Penguin Books, 1957), 210. For more on Teresa's *Life*, see Carlos Eire, *The Life of Saint Teresa of Avila:*

A Biography, Lives of Great Religious Books (Princeton, NJ, and Oxford: Princeton University Press, 2019).

37. On John's imprisonment, see Gerald Brenan, *St John of the Cross: His Life and Poetry* (London and New York: Cambridge University Press, 1973), 26–38.

38. The "Spiritual Canticle," as Colin P. Thompson points out, developed over a period of years. The bulk of the poem (up to stanza 31) was composed in prison between December 1577 and John's escape in August 1578. The final stanzas were added in 1582–1583. John also added prose expositions in 1578 or 1579. See Thompson, *The Poet and the Mystic: A Study of the Cántico Espiritual of San Juan de la Cruz* (Oxford: Oxford University Press, 1977), 21–32.

39. For more on the impact of Garcilaso de la Vega's poetry on John, see Dámaso Alonso, *La poesía de San Juan de la Cruz* (Madrid: Consejo Superior de Investigaciones Científicas, Instituto Antonio de Nebrija, 1942). Thompson regards Córdoba's mystical eclogues as another source of inspiration. See Thompson, *Poet and the Mystic*, 70–80.

40. John of the Cross, *The Spiritual Canticle of the Soul and the Bridegroom Christ*, trans. David Lewis (London: Thomas Baker, 1909), 2.

41. John of the Cross, "The Spiritual Canticle," trans. Colin P. Thompson, in Thompson, *Poet and the Mystic*, 173.

42. Thompson provides a list of phrases in the "Spiritual Canticle" that are indebted to the Vulgate's Latin translation of the Song; see Thompson, *Poet and the Mystic*, 62–65.

43. John of the Cross, "The Spiritual Canticle," in Thompson, *Poet and the Mystic*, 174.

44. John of the Cross, "The Spiritual Canticle," in Thompson, *Poet and the Mystic*, 175.

45. *John of the Cross: Selected Writings*, ed. Kieran Kavanaugh (New York: Paulist Press, 1987), 55–57.

46. Thompson, *Poet and the Mystic*, 28.

47. Quoted in the introduction to Manuel Durán and William Kluback, *Luis De Leon: The Names of Christ* (New York: Paulist Press, 1984), 23.

48. Quoted in Sheehan, *Enlightenment Bible*, 11–12.

49. See Jane Barr, "Luis de León and the Song of Songs," in *The Song of Songs: A Feminist Companion to the Bible*, ed. Athalya Brenner and Carole R. Fontaine (Sheffield, UK: Sheffield Academic Press, 2000), 130–141.

50. On Fray Luis's familiarity with the work of Ibn Ezra, see Luis M. Girón-Negrón," 'Your Dove-Eyes Among Your Hairlocks': Language and Authority in Fray Luis de León's *Respuesta que desde su prisión da a sus émulos*," *Renaissance Quarterly* 54 (2001), 1206.

51. On the history of Bible translations through the lens of Jewish-Christian difference, see Naomi Seidman, *Faithful Renderings: Jewish-Christian Difference and the Politics of Translation* (Chicago: Chicago University Press, 2006).

52. Quoted in Barr, "Luis de León," 138.

53. For an extensive consideration of Fray Luis's translation of Song 4:1, see Girón-Negrón, "'Your Dove-Eyes.'"

54. See appendix to Girón-Negrón,"'Your Dove-Eyes,'" 1242.

55. Quoted in Barr, "Luis de León," 134. John of the Cross may have been aware of Fray Luis's definition of the Song as an eclogue, but they could have reached the same conclusion independently given that the genre was popular during the Spanish Renaissance.

56. "*Una carta de amores sin ningún espíritu, y casa nada difiere de los amores de Ovidio*." Quoted in Thompson, *Strife of Tongues*, 60.

57. Quoted in Thompson, *Strife of Tongues*, 61. See Thompson's discussion of Fray Luis's exchange with Hernández on 61–62.

58. Fray Luis, *Cantar de los cantares de Salomón* (Salamanca: Ediciones Universidad de Salamanca, 2002), 25.

59. See Luis de León, *The Names of Christ* (New York: Paulist Press, 1984), esp. 239–262 ("Husband") and 325–343 ("Beloved").

60. Luis de León, *Names of Christ*, 39. For the full text of the dedication, see 35–40.

61. It is here, in his Latin exegesis, that Fray Luis's dialogue with Bernard is particularly extensive. See Thompson, *Strife of Tongues*, 104–109.

CHAPTER 4. Modern Scholars and the Quest for the Literal Song: From J. G. Herder to Phyllis Trible

1. Johann Gottfried von Herder, *Lieder der Liebe: die ältesten und schönsten aus Morgenlande, Nebst vier und vierzig alten Minneliedern, Sämmtliche Werke*, vol. 8 (Leipzig: Weygand, 1778), 485–588.

2. Quoted in Samuel Moyn's "Divine and Human Love: Franz Rosenzweig's History of the Song of Songs," *Jewish Studies Quarterly* 12 (2005): 200. Moyn's translation of Herder is based on the 1781 reprint of *Lieder der Liebe*.

3. Moyn, "Divine and Human Love," 200.

4. Sheehan, *Enlightenment Bible*, front flap and ix. For more on the Enlightenment Bible, see Stephen D. Moore and Yvonne Sherwood, *The Invention of the Biblical Scholar: A Critical Manifesto* (Minneapolis: Fortress Press, 2011).

5. It is noteworthy that Robert Lowth was Herder's English counterpart and another major founder of the literary approach to the Bible. Lowth offers an extensive account of the Song's aesthetic features in *De Poesi Sacrae Hebraeorum* (1753) but refuses to relinquish allegory as a viable mode of reading the Song. For a consideration of the interrelations between eighteenth-century German and English biblical criticism, see Robert T. Clark's, "Herder, Percy, and the Song of Songs," *PMLA* 61, no. 4 (1946): 1087–1100.

6. Quoted in John D. Baildam, *Paradisal Love: Johann Gottfried Herder and the Song of Songs* (Sheffield, UK: Sheffield Academic Press, 1999), 137.

7. For more on Herder's understanding of poetry and aesthetics beyond the biblical text, see Gregory Moore's introduction to *Selected Writings on Aesthetics: Johann Gottfried Herder*, trans. and ed. Gregory Moore (Princeton, NJ: Princeton University Press, 2006), 1–30.

8. Quoted in Baildam, *Paradisal Love*, 98.

9. See Baildam, *Paradisal Love*, 138.

10. Herder develops his notion of the Bible's oriental aesthetics in his *The Spirit of Hebrew Poetry*, trans. James Marsh (Burlington, VT: E. Smith, 1833).

11. Quoted in Hans W. Frei, *The Eclipse of Biblical Narrative: A Study in Eighteenth- and Nineteenth-Century Hermeneutics* (New Haven, CT: Yale University Press, 1974), 185.

12. Frei, *Eclipse of Biblical Narrative*, 185.

13. See Sheehan's consideration of the question of sympathy and distance in *The Enlightenment Bible*, 164–166.

14. Herder, *Lieder der Liebe, Die ältesten und schönsten aus Morgenlande. Nebst vier und vierzig alten Minneliedern* (Leipzig: Weygand, 1778), 12.

15. Quoted in Baildam, *Paradisal Love*, 186. Baildam provides an extensive discussion regarding the travel literature used by Herder in his commentary on the Song.

16. Moyn, "Divine and Human Love," 201.

17. Quoted in Baildam, *Paradisal Love*, 189.

18. Quoted in Baildam, *Paradisal Love*, 189.

19. Quoted in Baildam, *Paradisal Love*, 82–83.

20. Herder, "On German-Oriental Poets," in *Selected Early Works, 1764–1767: Addresses, Essays, and Drafts; Fragments on Recent German Literature*, ed. Ernest A. Menze and Karl Menges, trans. Ernest A. Menze and Michael Palma (University Park: Pennsylvania State University Press, 1992), 178.

21. For more on the national dimension of Herder's aesthetic project, see Baildam, *Paradisal Love*, 90–97; Sheehan, *Enlightenment Bible*, 168–173.

22. Wetzstein, "Die syrische Dreschtafel," *Zeitschrift für Ethnologie* 5 (1873): 270–301. Wetzstein's observations in this article are reprinted, with some additional remarks, in the appendix of Franz Delitzsch's commentary on the Song of Songs; see Delitzsch, *Commentary on the Song of Songs and Ecclesiastes*, trans. M. G. Easton (Eugene, OR: Wipf and Stock, 2009 [1885]).

23. The Arabic term *wasf* means "description."

24. See Delitzsch, *Commentary*, 170–176.

25. G. H. Dalman, *Palästinischer Diwan* (Leipzig: J. C. Hinrichs, 1901); S. H. Stephan, "Modern Palestinian Parallels to the Song of Songs," *JPOS* 2 (1922): 1–80.

26. Richard I. Cohen, "Urban Visibility and Biblical Visions: Jewish Culture in Western and Central Europe in the

Modern Age," in *Cultures of the Jews*, ed. David Biale (New York: Schocken Books, 2002), 762–786. For more on the Jewish Enlightenment, see Shmuel Feiner, *The Jewish Enlightenment*, trans. Chaya Naor (Philadelphia: University of Pennsylvania Press, 2002).

27. Tova Cohen, *Melitzat Yeshurun by Shlomo Löwisohn: The Work and Its Author* [in Hebrew] (Jerusalem: Bar Ilan University Press, 1988), 219.

28. Cohen, *Melitzat yeshurun*, 205.

29. Cohen, *Melitzat yeshurun*, 224–225. For more on Löwisohn, see Yosef Klausner, "Shlomo Levisohn (1789–1821)," in *The History of Modern Hebrew Literature* [in Hebrew] (Jerusalem: Ahiasaf, 1952), 1:261–274; and Tova Cohen's introduction to her *Melitzat yeshurun*.

30. Rosenzweig, *Star of Redemption*, 199.

31. In addition to Herder, Rosenzweig also criticizes Goethe, who endorsed a Herderian line in his translation of the Song. For a broader discussion of Rosenzweig's aesthetic-hermeneutic project, see Leora Batnitzky, *Idolatry and Representation: The Philosophy of Franz Rosenzweig Reconsidered* (Princeton, NJ: Princeton University Press, 2000).

32. Moyn, "Divine and Human Love," 198.

33. Rosenzweig, *Star of Redemption*, 200–201.

34. David Myers, *Resisting History: Historicism and Its Discontents in German-Jewish Thought* (Princeton, NJ, and Oxford: Princeton University Press, 2003).

35. See Moyn, "Divine and Human Love," 210–211. Note that Said devotes a brief section to the projection entailed in the quest through the contemporary Orient for biblical realities in his consideration of Holy Land travel narratives. See Edward Said, *Orientalism* (New York: Random House, 1978), 168.

36. Rosenzweig, *Star of Redemption*, 202.

37. Rosenzweig, *Star of Redemption*, 201.

38. T. J. Meek, "The Song of Songs and the Fertility Cult," in *A Symposium on the Song of Songs*, ed. W. H. Schoff (Philadelphia: n.p., 1924), 71–75.

39. Meek, "Song of Songs," 49.

40. The translation used by Meek in "Song of Songs," 62.

41. Meek, "Song of Songs," 62.

42. See Kramer, "The Biblical Song of Songs and Sumerian Love Songs, *Expedition* 5 (1969): 25–31; Kramer, *The Sacred Marriage Rite: Aspects of Faith, Myth, and Ritual in Ancient Sumer* (Bloomington: Indiana University Press, 1969), 85–106.

43. For a survey of the different studies of the cultic approach, see Pope, *Song of Songs*, 145–153.

44. Alter, *Art of Biblical Poetry*, 186.

45. Alter, *Art of Biblical Poetry*, 186.

46. Alter, *Art of Biblical Poetry*, 197.

47. Alter, *Art of Biblical Poetry*, 203. Another notable book that offers a literary approach to the Song is Francis Landy's *Paradoxes of Paradise: Identity and Difference in the Song of Songs* (Sheffield, UK: Sheffield Academic Press, 1983).

48. Phyllis Trible, "Depatriarchalizing in Biblical Interpretation," *Journal of the American Academy of Religion* 41 (March 1973): 30–48.

49. Trible, "Depatriarchalizing in Biblical Interpretation," 31.

50. See Trible, *God and the Rhetoric of Sexuality* (Philadelphia: Fortress Press, 1978), 159–160. The biblical translations are Trible's.

51. Trible, *God and the Rhetoric*, 161.

52. Trible, *God and the Rhetoric*, 158.

53. For a critique of Trible's approach, see Pardes, *Countertraditions in the Bible*, 20–25.

54. Athalya Brenner, ed., *A Feminist Companion to the Song of Songs* (Sheffield, UK: JSOT Press, 1993); and Athalya Brenner and Carole R. Fontaine, eds., *The Song of Songs: A Feminist Companion to the Bible* (Sheffield, UK: Sheffield Academic Press, 2000). Interestingly, Jane Barr's "Luis de León and the Song of Songs" appears in this later edition, as Fray Luis is regarded as a precursor of feminist criticism.

55. Kristeva, *Tales of Love*, 99–100.

56. Kristeva, *Tales of Love*, 99–100.

57. Kristeva, *Tales of Love*, 89.

58. Kristeva, *Tales of Love*, 90.

59. Kristeva, *Tales of Love*, 95

60. Kristeva, *Tales of Love*, 91.

61. Kristeva, *Tales of Love*, 90.

62. For more on Kristeva's postmodern readings of the Bible, see Elizabeth Castelli, Stephen D. Moore, Garry A. Phillips, and Regina M. Schwartz, *The Postmodern Bible: The Bible and Culture Collective* (New Haven, CT: Yale University Press, 1995), 211–222.

63. Although Kristeva does not mention Rosenzweig, her insistence on reconsidering the interrelations between human and divine love while setting them on the same footing may be indebted to *The Star of Redemption*.

CHAPTER 5. The Song of America: From Walt Whitman to Toni Morrison

1. The Song was not a key text in Puritan culture, but it did have some advocates, among them John Cotton, a leading pastor and writer. In *A Brief Exposition of the Whole Book of Canticles or Song of Solomon* (1642), Cotton provides an extensive allegorical reading of the Song as a prophetic account of church history, beginning with its early manifestations in Israel and the apostolic age to its reawakening in the Reformation. For more on Cotton's commentary on the Song, see Jeffrey A. Hammond, "The Bride in Redemptive Time: John Cotton and the Canticles Controversy," *New England Quarterly* 56, no. 1 (1983): 78–102.

2. See Lawrence Buell's chapter on "Literary Scripturism" in his *New England Literary Culture* (Cambridge: Cambridge University Press, 1986), 166–190.

3. Ezra Greenspan, ed., *Walt Whitman's Song of Myself: A Sourcebook and Critical Edition* (New York and London: Routledge, 2005), 55.

4. For more on Whitman's life and work, see David S. Reynolds, *Walt Whitman* (New York: Oxford University Press, 2005); Ed Folsom and Kenneth M. Price, "Walt Whitman," Walt Whitman Archive, https://whitmanarchive.org/biography/walt_whitman/index.html (accessed

November 16, 2018); Donald D. Kummings, ed., *A Companion to Walt Whitman* (Malden, MA, Oxford, and Victoria: Blackwell, 2006).

5. Elsewhere in *Leaves of Grass*, in "The Few Drops Known," Whitman explicitly refers to the "Hebrew canticles."

6. Citations from "Song of Myself" are from the Norton Critical Edition of *Leaves of Grass*, ed. Sculley Bradley and Harold W. Blodgett (New York: Norton, 1973).

7. Whitman calls attention to the admirable lack of meter and rhyming in biblical poetry in his essay "The Bible as Poetry," in *November Boughs* (1888), https://www.bartleby.com /229/5002.html (accessed November 16, 2018). For more on Whitman's biblicism, see Gay Wilson Allen, "Biblical Echoes in Whitman's Works," *American Literature* 6 (1934): 302–315; Thomas Becknell, "Bible," in *Walt Whitman: An Encyclopedia*, ed. J. R. LeMaster and Donald D. Kummings (New York: Garland, 1998), 55–56; Shira Wolosky Weiss, *Poetry and Public Discourse in Nineteenth-Century America* (New York: Palgrave Macmillan, 2010).

8. For a consideration of the Song's echoes in the opening lines of "Song of Myself," see Linda Munk, "Giving Umbrage: The Song of Songs Which Is Whitman's," *Journal of Literature and Theology* 7, no. 1 (March 1993), 50–65.

9. George R. Noyes's translation and commentary were among other things a response to Moses Stuart, the leading biblical scholar at Andover. Against Stuart, who advocated an allegorical reading of the text, Noyes argues that it would be "monstrous" to suggest that the biblical amatory poems are suitable for the representation of divine love. "There is language in the Canticles which I could not apply to the Supreme Being in the manner required by the mystical [i.e., allegorical] theory, without feeling guilty of blasphemy," he declares. George R. Noyes, *A New Translation of Job, Ecclesiastes, and the Canticles with Introductions and Notes, Chiefly Explanatory* (Boston: American Unitarian, 1868), 54.

10. See Munk, "Giving Umbrage," 53.

11. Whitman, "A Backward Glance O'er Travel'd Roads," in Sculley and Blodgett, *Leaves of Grass*, 574. On Whitman

and Herder, see Walter Grünzweig, "Herder," in *The Routledge Encyclopedia of Walt Whitman*, ed. J. R. LeMaster and Donald D. Kummings (New York and London: Routledge, 2011), 273.

12. See the discussion on the Shulamite's unique use of "I" in chapter 4.

13. Whitman, *Notes and Fragments*, ed. Richard Maurice Bucke (Ontario: A. Talbot & Co., 1899), part I, 170n.72, https://archive.org/details/fragmentleftwalt00whitrich/page/n173 (accessed November 16, 2018).

14. For more on Emerson's perception of allegory, see Deborah L. Madsen, "American Allegory to 1900," in Copeland and Struck, *Cambridge Companion to Allegory*, 229–240.

15. Ed Folsom, *Song of Myself with a Complete Commentary* (Iowa City: University of Iowa Press, 2016).

16. Whitman, Introduction to *Leaves of Grass* (1885), reprinted in the Norton Critical Edition, 713–714.

17. Herman Melville, *Correspondence*, ed. Lynn Horth (Evanston, IL: Northwestern University Press, 1993), 192.

18. Melville, *Correspondence*, 483. *Clarel* first appeared in an edition of 350 copies (thanks to the financial support of Melville's uncle, Peter Gansevoort), of which about a third were sold and the rest pulped three years later.

19. For more on the reception of the book, see Hershel Parker, *Herman Melville: A Biography*, vol. 2, *1851–1981* (Baltimore and London: Johns Hopkins University Press, 2002), 790–814.

20. For more on *Clarel* and the Song of Songs, see Ilana Pardes, "Melville's Song of Songs: *Clarel* as Aesthetic Pilgrimage," in *Melville and Aesthetics*, ed. Samuel Otter and Geoffrey Sanborn (New York: Palgrave, 2011), 213–233.

21. Stan Goldman provides an illuminating reading of Melville's debt to Psalms but overlooks the pivotal role of the Song. See his *Melville's Protest Theism: The Hidden and Silent God in* Clarel (DeKalb: Northern Illinois University Press), 1993.

22. Howard C. Horsford with Lynn Horth, eds., *The Writings of Herman Melville*, vol. 15, *Journals* (Evanston, IL, and

Chicago: Northwestern University Press and the Newberry Library, 1989), 91.

23. On Melville's reflections on America's biblical heritage in *Clarel*, see Hilton Obenzinger, *American Palestine: Melville, Twain, and the Holy Land Mania* (Princeton, NJ: Princeton University Press, 1999).

24. Harrison Hayford, Alma A. MacDougall, Hershel Parker, and G. Thomas Tanselle, eds., *The Writings of Herman Melville*, vol. 12, *Clarel: A Poem and Pilgrimage into the Holy Land* (Evanston, IL, and Chicago: Northwestern University Press and the Newberry Library, 1991). All future citations are from this edition.

25. Herman Melville, *Correspondence*, ed. Lynn Horth (Evanston, IL: Northwestern University Press, 1993), 191.

26. On Vine as the embodiment of Hawthorne, see Walter E. Bezanson, "Historical and Critical Note," in Hayford et al., *Clarel*, 593–604. On the homoerotic quality of Clarel's bond with Vine, see Nina Baym, "The Erotic Motif in Melville's *Clarel*," *Texas Studies in Literature and Language* 16, no. 2 (1974): 315–328.

27. *Memoirs of the Life, Religious Experience, Ministerial Travels and Labours of Mrs. Zilpha Elaw, an American Female of Colour* (London: Published by the authoress, and sold by T. Dudley, 1846), 51. See Katherine Clay Bassard's discussion of Zilpha Elaw's use of the Song in her *Transforming Scriptures: African American Women Writers and the Bible* (Athens and London: University of Georgia Press, 2010). Frederick Douglass, "A Tribute for the Negro; Being a Vindication of the Moral and Religious Capabilities, of the Colored Portion of Mankind; with Particular Reference to the African Race," *North Star* (Rochester, NY), April 7, 1849; Hannah Craft, *The Bondwoman's Narrative by Hannah Craft, a Fugitive Slave Recently Escaped from North Carolina* [ca. 1853–1861], https://brbl-dl.library.yale.edu /vufind/Record/3520207 (accessed November 14, 2018).

28. W.E.B. Du Bois, *The Souls of Black Folk* (New York: Signet, 1969 [1903]), 140.

29. *My Soul's High Song: The Collected Writings of Countee Cullen, Voice of the Harlem Renaissance*, ed. Gerald Early (New York: Doubleday, 1991), 201.

30. Langston Hughes, *The First Book of Negroes* (New York: F. Watts, 1952), 23.

31. Indebted as Morrison is to the great resonance of the King James Version in African American literature (from slave spirituals to the novels of Zora Neale Hurston and James Baldwin) and in American literature as a whole, she chooses to adhere to the title of the KJV translation—Song of Solomon—rather than to the more accurate translation of *shir ha-shirim*: Song of Songs. For more on the resonance of the KJV in American literature, see Robert Alter, *Pen of Iron: American Prose and the King James Bible* (Princeton, NJ: Princeton University Press, 2010).

32. Toni Morrison, *Song of Solomon* (New York: Signet, 1977), 5. All future citations are from this edition and will be given in parentheses in the text.

33. Much like the biblical Hagar, Morrison's Hagar is abandoned and rejected. What is more, given that the biblical Hagar was a slave, she has a special resonance in the context of American slavery. It is no coincidence that one of the female slaves in Harriet Beecher Stowe's *Uncle Tom's Cabin* is called Hagar.

34. For a reading of the lovemaking of Milkman and Sweet as a celebration of the Song of Songs, see Judy Pocock, "'Through a Glass Darkly': Typology in Toni Morrison's *Song of Solomon*," *Canadian Review of American Studies* 35, no. 3 (2005): 281–298, 285.

35. Du Bois, *Souls of Black Folk*, 265.

36. Savannah Unit, Georgia Writers' Project, *Drums and Shadows: Survival Studies Among the Georgia Coastal Negroes* (Athens: University of Georgia Press, 1940). The African tales and songs of *Drums and Shadows* were collected in the 1930s. On Morrison's use of this work, see Therese E. Higgins, *Religiosity, Cosmology, and Folklore: The African Influence in the Novels of Toni Morrison* (New York and London: Routledge, 2001), 5–28.

37. Quoted in Higgins, *Religiosity, Cosmology, and Folklore*, 9.

38. Toni Morrison, *Beloved* (New York: Penguin Books, 1987), 5. All future citations are to this edition and will be given in parentheses in the text.

39. For more on this polyphonic sequence, see Homi Bhabha, *Location of Culture* (London and New York: Routledge, 1994), 17; Christopher Peterson, "Beloved's Claim," in *Toni Morrison's* Beloved, Bloom's Modern Critical Interpretations Series (new ed.), ed. Harold Bloom (New York: Infobase, 2009), 151–172.

40. Quoted in Higgins, *Religiosity, Cosmology, and Folklore*, 5.

41. For a consideration of the allegorical underpinning of the move to the South in *Song of Solomon*, see Pocock, "'Through a Glass Darkly,'" 286–287.

42. On the mixture of personal and collective experiences in slave religion, see Albert J. Raboteau, *Slave Religion: The "Invisible Institution" in the Antebellum South* (Oxford and New York: Oxford University Press, 1978), esp. 245–247.

43. For more on Morrison's renditions of the Song, see Ilana Pardes, "Morrison's New Shulamites: The African-American Song," in *Remapping Feminist Criticism*, ed. Yvonne Sherwood (Oxford, UK: Oxford University Press, 2017), 133–149.

44. The prayer was delivered at St. Lydia's Dinner Church for the "This Is My Body Series" in September 2015 and posted on the "Wholeness4all" website shortly afterward: https://wholeness4all.wordpress.com/2015/10/05/dark-and-lovely-the-call-to-love-the-black-womans-body/ (accessed August 9, 2016).

45. Micky ScottBey Jones, "I Am Black and Beautiful," *SheLovesMagazine.com*, March 24, 2016, http://shelovesmagazine.com/2016/i-am-black-and-beautiful/ (accessed August 10, 2016). For additional examples of such rhetoric, see Douglas M. Donley, "Black Is Beautiful," sermon delivered at University Baptist Church, Minneapolis, MN, September 27, 2015, http://www.ubcmn.org/sundays/sermons/item/760-september-27-2015 (accessed October 16, 2018); and "Black Lives Matter to God!," Verity

& Charity Publications, July 27, 2016, https://veritycharity
.com/blogs/news/black-lives-matter-to-god (accessed
October 18, 2017).

46. Macy Gray, "Toni Morrison," Black Lives Matter, May 15,
2016, sayhername.blacklivesmatter.com/toni-morrison
(accessed October 16, 2018).

EPILOGUE: "Flee My Lover and Be Like a Deer or Like a Gazelle on the Spice Mountains"

1. Some readers attribute these aphorisms to the Shulamite,
but the shift in tone and genre and lack of direct address to
the lover make it difficult to determine the speaker's identity.

2. This genre is the predominant mode of discourse in Proverbs.
For a comparison between the aphorisms of the Song and
those of Proverbs, see Zakovitch, *Shir HaShirim*, 133–135.

3. The anxiety of scorn is also evident earlier in the chapter:
"Would that you were a brother to me, / suckling my
mother's breasts. / I would find you in the street, would kiss
you, / and they would show no scorn for me" (8:1).

4. See Alter, *Art of Biblical Poetry*, 195.

5. Anna Ruth Henriques' work on the Song of Songs includes
eight paintings—one for each chapter of the ancient love
poem: see http://www.henriquesart.com/song-of-songs
?lightbox=image20m.

6. S. Y. Agnon, "And Solomon's Wisdom Excelled," trans.
Mordechai Beck, with minor revisions, *Ariel—Israel Review
of Arts and Letters 92* (1993), 278–279. For more on Agnon's
tale, see Pardes, *Agnon's Moonstruck Lovers: The Song of
Songs in Israeli Culture*, Samuel and Althea Stroum Lectures
in Jewish Studies (Seattle and London: University of Washington Press, 2013), 17–21.

7. Agnon, "And Solomon's Wisdom Excelled," 278–279.

8. Agnon, "And Solomon's Wisdom Excelled," 279.

A page number in italics refers to a figure or its caption.

Ben Azzai, 38–42, 235n25
Benjamin, Walter, 26
Ben Zoma, 41, 235n25
Bernard de Clairvaux, 99–110;
on divine breasts, 119;
evoked by Melville's *Clarel*,
192; evoked in Melville's
Clarel, 191; Fray Luis and,
111, 112, 134, 248n61; John of
the Cross and, 110–11, 112,
123, 126; Kristeva and, 169;
opening kiss and, 100, 102–5;
Origen's *Commentary* and,
100–101, 103; praising artfulness of the Song, 139; *Sermones* of, 100–110, 111; sixteenth-century Spanish
mysticism influenced by, 111,
112; spiritual affect and, 105–
10; Teresa of Ávila and, 110–
11, 112
Bernini, Gian Lorenzo, 120–21;
The Ecstasy of Saint Teresa,
121, *122*
Bible. *See* literary approach to
the Bible; translations of the
Bible
"black but comely," 196; Morrison's evocations of, 201–2,
204, 215; translations using
"and comely," 197–98, 216–17
"Black is beautiful," 197–98, 216
Black Lives Matter movement,
216–18, 223
"Black Majesty" (Cullen), 197
bodily experiences: as part of
many allegorical readings, 17;
of Teresa of Ávila, 120–21;

Whitman's poetry capturing
the joy of, 177, 180. *See also*
sexuality in the Song
body: in ecstasy of Teresa of
Ávila, 118–21; Ezekiel's vision
of divine body, 42; growing
emphasis on, 18–19, 103–4;
highlighted in the opening
kiss, 103; humanity of Christ
and, 104; Origen's condem-
nation of, 53; Song's bold
celebration of, 20; tangible in
Bernard's sermons, 103–4;
Whitman's affirmation of,
177
The Bondwoman's Narrative
(Craft), 196
breasts: of the Bridegroom,
Teresa of Ávila on, 118–20;
compared to fawns, 22, 23,
62, 150, 222; in Ezekiel's marital metaphor, 28, 29; in Ibn
Ezra's literary metaphor, 62–
63; in Ibn Gabirol's liturgical
poetry, 78, 79; in John's
"Spiritual Canticle," 128; like
towers, proclaimed by
Shulamite, 179, 202; mis-
translation of the Hebrew for
"love" as, 118, 132, 246n28; as
Moses and Aaron in *Song of
Songs Rabba*, 22, 23; mountains as metaphor for, 219;
Origen and Bernard on di-
vine breasts, 119
Brenner, Athalya, 166
Bride: as Church in Origen's
allegorical world, 46–50,

exegesis, 12, 27, 28, 31, 37, 48, 94; mystical world of Zohar and, 84, 94; Shulamite as appealing role for, 31. *See also* Jerusalem

companions, Zoharic, 91, 92, 93

conversos, 112, 131, 245n17

Córdoba, Sebastiàn de, 124

Cordovero, Moses, 243n54

Cotton, John, 253n1

Counter-Reformation, 111–12, 118

courtly love literature, in medieval France, 100

Craft, Hannah, 196

Cullen, Countee, 197, 207

cultic approach, 19, 156–60; Alter's criticism of, 162; riddle of canonization and, 15

Dalman, G. H., 151

Dante, 99

"Dark Night of the Soul" (Saint John of the Cross), 128–29

daughters of Jerusalem, 6–7; Agnon's story referring to, 228; in fragmentary final chapter of the Song, 220; Ibn Gabirol's poetry and, 79; Morrison's possible echo of, 213; Shulamite's cautionary words to, 228, 229; Teresa's *hijas* cast in role of, 116, 246n24; Trible's feminist interpretation and, 165

deer: Arabic ghazăl as, 64; imperative to be like, 219–20, 221–22; midrashic

interpretation of, 71–72. *See also* doe; fawns; hart; roe; stag

"Depatriarchalizing in Biblical Interpretation" (Trible), 164

derasha (midrashic mode of exegesis), 87–88, 241n42

dialogue upon handles of the lock, 8–10; Ibn Gabirol's poetry and, 76–79; Melville's *Clarel* and, 193; parable in the Zohar and, 86–88, 90

The Divine Comedy (Dante), 99

divine love: Bernard's attention to, 109–10; canonization of the Song and, 12–13; cultic approach and, 157; Enlightenment scholarship uninterested in, 136–37; esoteric sites of, in *Song of Songs Rabba*, 41; "Hymn to the Sabbath" and, 96–97; Kristeva on Song's explorations of, 167, 169; medieval Hebrew liturgical poetry and, 71–72, 74–79; Melville's *Clarel* and, 195; monastic exegetes and, 98–99; Noyes' literalist-aesthetic approach and, 254n9; polytheistic paradigms of divine *eros* and, 12; in predominant allegorical reading of Song, 16; Rosenzweig on human love in relation to, 154–55; Shekhinah and, 84; Teresa on intoxication of, 121; Whitman's sexual interpretation of, 180–82. *See also* love

interpretation, 229; Herder's vision of the East and, 142; Ibn Ezra's use of, 62–63; Kristeva on amorous discourse and, 168–69; plethora of, in the Song, 4–6; prophetic marital metaphor, 12–13, 28–31, 45–48, 213–14

Michaelis, Johann David, 144

midrashic commentaries, 27–43; Agnon's story building on, 225–26; chronology of, 27; as composite verse-by-verse commentary, 27–28; prophetic marital metaphor and, 12–13, 28–31; as source for liturgical poetry of al-Andalus, 60; Zohar's debt to, 60, 82–83, 90. *See also* Akiva, Rabbi; *Song of Songs Rabba*

Moby-Dick (Melville), 185, 192

monasticism, Christian: asceticism in, 53, 98; medieval (*see* Bernard de Clairvaux); sixteenth-century Spanish, 110–12 (*see also* John of the Cross, Saint; León, Luis de; Teresa of Ávila, Santa)

moon: Shekhinah represented by, 85–86, 90–92, 93; Shulamite as, 149; in Song of Songs, 86

Morrison, Toni, 19, 172–74, 198–218; affirming her belief in ghosts, 212; *Beloved*, 19, 198, 209–16, 218; feminist potentiality of the Song and, 198–99, 203; folkloric quality of the Song and, 206; as

mentor of Black Lives Matter movement, 218; *Song of Solomon*, 19, 198–209, *199*, 218

Moshe de León, 82, 240n31

mother's house: in Morrison's *Beloved*, 211–12; in the Song, 109, 165

Mount Sinai: chariot mysticism and, 38–40; Ezekiel's marital metaphor and, 29, 34; midrashic commentators on Song's hart and, 72; Rabbi Akiva and, 33–34, 39; rabbinic disputes over dating of the Song and, 32, 85; rabbinic responses to Origen and, 56–57

mystical exegesis of late antiquity, 24; Origen's drama of the soul and, 50; in *Shi'ur Koma*, 42, 45; traces in *Song of Songs Rabba*, 37–43

mystical exegetes: Bernard de Clairvaux as, 99, 191; defining Song as nuptial song, 148; Jewish (*see* Zohar); monastic, 98–99; Rosenzweig's critique of Herder and, 154; seeking experiential knowledge of God, 37–38, 40; sixteenth-century Spanish, 110–12 (*see also* John of the Cross, Saint; León, Luis de; Teresa of Ávila, Santa). *See also* mystical exegesis of late antiquity

Najara, Israel, 96

The Name of the Rose (Eco), 98, 243n1

language and subjectivity of, 166–67; in Löwisohn's triangular drama, 152–53; Melville's Vine in position of, 193; Morrison's Beloved as, 214; Morrison's fascination with assertive voice and daring eroticism of, 199, 203; Morrison's Hagar as, 203–4, 257n33; Morrison's Pilate and, 200–201, 203, 208–9; as name of the beloved, 4; origin of name, 232n6; Teresa of Ávila casting herself in role of, 116; Trible's feminist interpretation of, 165. *See also* beloved

slave narratives, 195

slavery: of the Israelites in Egypt, 29; Morrison's *Beloved* and, 198, 209, 211, 212, 214, 215, 257n33; Morrison's *Song of Solomon* and, 198, 208

sod (mystical mode of exegesis), 88, 241n42

Solomon: Herder on authorship of the Song and, 139–40; reputation of, 3; traditional authorship of the Song and, 3–4; in triangular drama, 152–53, 168; Zohar on origin of the Song and, 84–86

"Song of Myself" (Whitman), 68, 174–79, 180–82, 183–84

Song of Solomon (Morrison), 19, 198–209, *199*; Black Lives Matter movement and, 218

Song of Songs: as anthology of love poems, 3–4, 10–11;

aphorisms in final chapter of, 220–21, 259nn1–3; arbitrary division into chapters, 7; canonization of, 11–16, 20; in contemporary culture, 223; dates of origin, 3–4; editors of, 3–4, 10–11; musical adaptations of, 13–14; Origen on the title of, 46–47; popularity of, 13–14; as Song of Solomon in King James Version, 257n31; spatial fluidity of, 41; suite of paintings based on, 223, *224*, 259n5

Song of Songs Rabba, 18, 27–43; allegorical gazelles in, 71–72; breasts like fawns interpreted in, 22; chronology of, 27; emphasizing Red Sea or Mount Sinai, 32, 85 (*see also* Mount Sinai; Red Sea); linking each verse to scenes of Exodus, 31–32, 33–37; possible responses to Origen in, 56–58; *Rabba* meaning "great," 233n7; sources of, 233n8, 235n25; traces of mysticism in, 37–43. *See also* Akiva, Rabbi

Song of the Sea, 36, 48, 234n19

soul: as Bride in Bernard's nuptial allegory, 100–101, 105–6, 107–8, 109; as Bride in John's "Spiritual Canticle," 123, 125–28, 129; Neoplatonic interpreters and, 24, 25, 49–50; Neoplatonic philosophy of Ibn Gabirol and, 79–80; Origen's drama of, 49–52,

soul (*continued*)
100–101; Teresa on intoxication of, 119–20; translations of the Bible and, 106–7; Whitman's poetry addressed to, 180, 181, 182
"Soul's Beloved" (Azikri), 96
The Souls of Black Folk (Du-Bois), 196, 206
Spanish Renaissance: Fray Luis de León and, 135; pastoral poetry of, 123–24, 248n55
The Spirit of Hebrew Poetry (Herder), 140, 143
"Spiritual Canticle" (Saint John of the Cross), 123–29, 247n38
stag: as common component of eclogues, 125; Ibn Ezra's imagery drawing on, 63; as key metaphor in the Song, 65, 66, 71–72; as lover in John's "Spiritual Canticle," 125–26; lover peering through the window as, 8; lover's abundance of roles including, 149; as Messiah in Ibn Gabirol's poetry, 78
The Star of Redemption (Rosen-zweig), 153–56, 253n63
Stephan, S. H., 151
Stuart, Moses, 254n9
Sumerian parallels with the Song, 159
sun: as the beloved in medieval Hebrew love poetry, 69–70; Shulamite as, 149

symbol: allegory and, 26, 89; Scholem on Zohar and, 88–89

Tales of Love (Kristeva), 166–67
Tannaitic sages, 27, 28, 32; supposed origin of Zohar and, 81. *See also* Akiva, Rabbi
Temple, and origin of the Song in the Zohar, 85
Teresa of Ávila, Santa, 110–11, 112, 113–22; Bernini's sculpture *The Ecstasy of Saint Teresa*, 121, *122*; breasts of the Bridegroom and, 118–20; canonization of, 121–22; definitive edition of 1588 prepared by Fray Luis, 130; on "dying of love," 120, 246n34; egalitarian construction of love in the Song and, 166; as first female exegete of the Song, 113; Fray Luis and, 130, 134; Inquisition and, 112, 113, 115, 116, 245n23; Kristeva and, 169; *Meditations on the Song of Songs*, 113–20, 121, 126, 181; Saint John of the Cross and, 123, 126; Whitman's ecstatic experience compared to, 181–82
"That Night a Gazelle" (Ha-Levi), 69–70
Thompson, Colin P., 129, 245n18, 247nn38–39, 247n42
Tish'a be-Av, 72, 242n44

Yohanan, Rabbi, 57
Yose, Rabbi, 84–85